# Pope Francis:
## Our Brother, Our Friend

# Pope Francis:
# Our Brother, Our Friend

as revealed in interviews
edited and translated by

Alejandro Bermúdez

IGNATIUS PRESS    SAN FRANCISCO

Cover art:
*Cardinal Jorge Bergoglio outside San Cayetano Church in
Buenos Aires, Friday August 7, 2009*
Associated Press photo / Natacha Pisarenko. © AP Images

Cover design by John Herreid

ISBN 978-1-58617-872-7
Library of Congress Control Number 2013936877
Printed in the United States of America ♾

# Contents

# Introduction

The first Jesuits arrived in what is now Argentina from Peru in November 1585 and settled in the city of Córdoba, where they have had a very important presence to this day. There they created the first university in the country and provided the human and spiritual force necessary to evangelize the surrounding areas, which included the famous "Reducciones" of Paraguay, immortalized in the movie *The Mission*. Their presence in Buenos Aires, today's cosmopolitan capital of Argentina, was not significant until the Society returned to Argentina on August 9, 1863, following their suppression and subsequent restoration. In the midst of the instability and violent political history of the country, the Jesuits managed to establish themselves firmly in Buenos Aires, and in 1938 the Argentinean Province was born with 324 Jesuits, separated from Chile.

The community of San Miguel, on the outskirts of the city of Buenos Aires, then became the "Colegio Máximo de San José", the formation center for the Jesuit vocations coming from Argentina, Bolivia, Uruguay, and Paraguay.

Hundreds of Jesuits, arriving to be formed as priests or brothers, have traveled through the large grove that leads to the Colegio Máximo's front door. In 1958, a thin young man, a technician in chemistry, the son of an immigrant from Piedmont, in northern Italy, traveled through that same grove. His name was Jorge Mario Bergoglio, and neither he nor his peers imagined that this young man would one day become the first Jesuit pope and the first pope from America.

Pope Francis, with his simple style and his direct manner of preaching, with its touch of humor, is a living image of his country, Argentina. Yet his spirituality clearly reflects that of Saint Ignatius, who has inspired and nourished him during most—and the most decisive—part of his life.

The young Bergoglio entered the diocesan seminary of Buenos Aires when it was still run by the Jesuits, and, after one year, he discovered in his professors of formation the path to which he was being called: that of the Society of Jesus.

On March 11, 1958, he entered the novitiate of the Society of Jesus. He completed his humanities studies in Chile, and in 1963 he went back to Argentina. He graduated with a degree in philosophy from the Colegio Máximo in San Miguel.

Between 1964 and 1965, he was professor of literature and psychology at the La Inmaculada school in Santa Fe and in 1966 taught the same subjects at the school of El Salvador in Buenos Aires, which would later evolve into a Catholic university.

From 1967 to 1970, he studied theology at the Colegio Máximo.

He was ordained a priest on December 13, 1969, and continued his formation in Spain between 1970 and 1971. On April 22, 1973, he made his perpetual profession as a Jesuit. Again in Argentina, he was master of novices at the Novitiate of San Ignacio as well as consultant for the province for the Society of Jesus and vice rector of the Colegio Máximo.

On July 13, 1973, he was elected the youngest provincial of the Jesuits, a position that he held in Argentina until the end of 1979. Between 1980 and 1986, he became the rector of the Colegio Máximo San José and was also a pastor in San Miguel.

In March 1986, he traveled to Germany to do his doctoral thesis on Romano Guardini, which he never finished.

In 1987, his superiors sent him to the school of El Salvador in Buenos Aires and, in 1991, to the Jesuit residence of the Society of Jesus in Córdoba, where he served as a professor, spiritual director, and confessor.

In 1992 he was named auxiliary bishop of Buenos Aires. He was ordained a bishop by Cardinal Antonio Quarracino, then archbishop of Buenos Aires, on June 27. In June 1997, he was named coadjutor archbishop, and, on February 28, 1998, he took possession of the archdiocese—the primatial see of Argentina.

The relationship of the current Pope Francis with his community was not always easy. Some moments of his life as a Jesuit, especially his term of office as provincial and the reason for his transfer to Córdoba, are interpreted in diverse ways by the brothers of his congregation. Here we have collected the testimonies of ten Argentinean Jesuits who lived close to Father Bergoglio, some as professors, others as peers, and others as his disciples. When they refer to the Jesuits in these interviews, they will often use "the Society".

Yet, the personality of the current pope would remain incomplete if it were not enriched with the testimony of other people, from the important politician to the beggar and from the rabbi to the priest working in the slums of Buenos Aires.

The interviews were made possible by the meticulous work of my colleague and friend Walter Sánchez Silva, news editor for the agency ACI Prensa in Lima, Peru, and they were conducted one month after the election of Pope Francis. The interviews vary in length and depth, depending upon the disposition of the person interviewed. Different interviewees naturally gravitated to different issues.

Because these are interviews—first-person accounts— there may be occasional differences in the details or opinions these individuals relate about events that occurred involving Pope Francis, but they essentially transmit a mosaic that reveals little-known aspects of the pontiff's personality, of his interior world, his human abilities, his work habits, his devotions, his concerns, and his friendships. And, thus, they open a fascinating door to a better understanding of the man whom the Holy Spirit has elected to conduct the Church at this time.

# Father Carlos Carranza, S.J.

(eighty-eight years old and the third oldest member of the Argentinean Jesuit Province)

*What characterizes a Jesuit like Bergoglio?*

The key to understanding our vocation is the Spiritual Exercises of Saint Ignatius, the spiritual experience of Saint Ignatius. We receive it, we assimilate it, and so on, and we imitate it when we do our Spiritual Exercises upon entering the Society, when we do one month of Spiritual Exercises. But our experience also depends a lot upon our spiritual fathers, upon our superiors, who are the ones who guide us.

*How did you know Father Bergoglio?*

I knew him personally, something that's not necessarily a given, because when I entered, there were more than two hundred Jesuits in the Argentinean Province. I am not going to be very specific with regard to dates. The first time I met Bergoglio was when I was the spiritual prefect in the Santa Fe Province, in the Inmaculada school. He was a regent, and from that first moment he seemed to be mature: he was discreet, serene, peaceful; someone for whom the students cared a lot.

He was a professor of literature, something very interesting, because besides the natural speaking qualities he has, he also adds a literary knowledge that gives him the ability to explain things in a very beautiful way, and a way that is also very enjoyable to listen to. For example, his homily for the Chrism Mass on Holy Saturday (2013) reflects the poetic touch of his speech. As spiritual prefect, I was concerned with the spiritual formation of the students while he had to look after a department of the school, during a time when we had students who were residents, organized into five divisions.

This information today may seem superfluous, but we know that God has a plan, that God chooses like he chose Abraham or John the Baptist; and like he chose Pope Francis, and for this plan he prepares us through the different phases of life.

Saint Ignatius has taught us that we have to use discernment in the face of the difficult situations of our life: discernment. What does discernment mean? It means looking at the positive and negative aspects of each situation in which we live and deciding what will be our response in accordance with the plan of God. And I believe that Bergoglio has demonstrated a great capacity for discernment in the different responsibilities the Society has given him.

For example, when he was master of novices. The master of the novices among us is a person chosen by the provincial as one who is sufficiently prepared to guide those who enter the Society of Jesus. Bergoglio was a person who could intuitively discover the qualities of each person who entered and draw on the natural inclinations of the candidate to help him become a good priest.

He also showed this capacity for discernment in a gracious and prudent way when he served as provincial. When he was provincial, I was in Belgium, and he went to visit me, despite the fact that it was a very hard time for him because of what was happening in Argentina (during the military government) and despite the fact that he suffered a lot during that time.

These visits that he made were very paternal and close. He encouraged me a lot to learn and to improve, so that I could be more effective in my apostolate and in my mission. And he always maintained that closeness. Even later, when I didn't see him much for three years, during a large meeting of clergy, more than five hundred priests, he saw me, and he recognized me immediately and said to me: Negro!— because they called me the Negro Carranza—"What's up? How's it going? How are you? What are you doing?" As always, he was very concerned about each person.

*How were Father Bergoglio's first years as provincial?*

Those years were very difficult for everyone, especially for him. It must be understood that he had a mind-set, a plan. He had great gifts for governing: faith, wisdom, and cleverness, that is, astuteness. But, well, not everyone agreed with that plan. Every person has the freedom to dissent, and many had dissented from him in some things that he had determined internally and also in terms of their attitudes regarding the social problems and the politics during that time.

I know that those confrontations caused Bergoglio to suffer a lot and that there were many who did not approve, who did not agree with the way he governed the province at that time. That is as much as I am able to say. We should not go into specific cases.

*And how were the years that followed his period as provincial?*

Immediately after being provincial, he became rector of the Colegio Máximo in San Miguel, where we study before becoming ordained as priests. It was an important time as one in charge of formation, but after that, there came a time when it seemed that he was going to devote himself exclusively to meditation. He was here in Córdoba during those years, and it was surprising to us; we thought he might be sick. He did not want to dedicate himself exclusively to prayer, but he remained faithful in the Society; because if he was going to dedicate himself solely to prayer, he could have gone elsewhere. But he remained faithful as a Jesuit. That is the Providence of God. At that time, Cardinal (Antonio) Quarracino sought out Jorge to give him the Spiritual Exercises. I know that the cardinal was very impressed with his spirituality and, at the same time, had known him as a leader and administrator.

And that's why Quarracino proposed that he become the auxiliary bishop of Buenos Aires. Later, he made him his coadjutor, and later he became archbishop of Buenos Aires. And, well, we jump ahead to the thirteenth of the third month of the year thirteen, and he becomes Pope Francis.

*And what is the reaction of the Jesuits?*

I am very satisfied, joyful for what this means. I know that there are Jesuits for whom it is going to be a bit difficult to assimilate the fact that their provincial or their rector at this moment is the Vicar of Christ. One has to remember that the pope is a Jesuit with all of his heart. The letter he wrote Father General Adolfo Nicolás indicates that he continues to appreciate the Society a lot; he speaks of his dear Society of Jesus.

Because he appreciates the institution, I believe he is always going to have recourse to us, but it's clear that for now relations are going to be diplomatic.

*Everyone knows the anecdote about when Pope Francis called the Jesuit Generalate in Rome and a novice answered the phone. When the secretary of the Father General tells the pope that they are praying for him, the pope asks him, "Are you praying that I go forward or backward?"*

Like I said, he manages his words very well, and he knows how to take advantage of situations. He is very clever. I thank God he has been elected, and I ask him to give him sufficient grace and wisdom to be able to govern the Church.

I think it is Providence that has put him there. This has been the culmination of his path as a priest and as a Jesuit. I never believed that this, something so extraordinary, would happen for the Society of Jesus. Little by little in the Society we shall assimilate this.

God willing, the Lord will really be able to achieve unity in the Church and in the world with all the prayers that are being lifted up for Francis. This would be the principal legacy that Pope Francis could leave us.

# Father Fernando Cervera, S.J.

(fifty years old, whose spiritual adviser was Father Bergoglio)

*How did you meet Father Bergoglio, now Pope Francis?*

I met him when I was an adolescent, because he was the provincial of the Society here in Argentina, and I was a student at the Colegio Jesuita in Santa Fe. But, at the same time, my mother was very close to him because they knew each other when my mother was working in the school; he started to study English with her. And I had contact with him upon entering the Society of Jesus in 1980. At various times he was one of those in charge of my formation during the stage of studies and of spiritual formation. Some years later he also became the person who guided me spiritually, and he did so for many years.

*What memory do you have from those years of formation as a Jesuit?*

Many. Bergoglio's personality and his way of directing the process of formation were very strong, and it was very difficult to be indifferent in his company. To give you an example: he was a person who went from giving spiritual assistance to someone to speaking on the phone with a bishop or some important person to washing clothes in the laundry or to the kitchen or where they raised the "hogs", as we called the pigs, and then later went back to see what was going on in the classroom—and he was involved in every detail with each one of us.

At the same time, he was a person who was permanently concerned about the individual process and the personal situation of each person. Bergoglio, at this time, had a deep impact on our formation because he was very demanding about our studies, our spiritual life, and our community life. It was a process that he modified from year to year.

He lived personally and explicitly instilled a religious vision in us of reality. He did not teach that our vocation should respond to an ideology or a sociological vision but, rather, that it was a call to serve Christ.

I remember, also, that at that time this provoked, on the one hand, a lot of respect, a lot of support; but in some people in the province it also caused a lot of rejection.

*What were his years like as provincial?*

As provincial, he helped the Society come back from a very strong crisis after the Second Vatican Council. As elsewhere around the world and in the whole Society, after the Council there were different trials that provoked many unfortunate exits. As provincial, he actively worked to save many Jesuits who were very affected by this crisis, and he promoted a lot of prayer, work, and vocations.

It was shortly after this that he took on the task of formation faced with an avalanche of vocations that, honestly, could have gone in any direction. He gave formation his personal imprint. As is well known, he was provincial during a very difficult period for the country. So, any intervention of his was going to be polemical anyway. But his period as the one in charge of formation, in which he was in charge of my formation, was after he was provincial, after he had generated an avalanche of vocations.

*What was he like in guiding formation?*

He created an external framework of a very open schedule, where he set aside the early morning for prayer. He fundamentally instilled great personal freedom. His method was to say: "This is the suggestion; you choose what you are going to do, but do so knowing that this interior discipline, this practice, or that spiritual reading serves this purpose." There was a priority on the spiritual, obviously, as there continues to be and as there always has been in the Society. So, everything that was experienced was brought to that spiritual dialogue and prayer and, well, what is most appropriate for the Society, discernment. That is to say, every process of decision making and choice had to be brought to the interior to see what motivations there were. This marked not only prayer, moreover, but also action. There was a requirement to work on certain personal issues that arose during formation by means of a discipline of duty. For example, if it makes me better, even though it is harder for me, a particular duty, we would dedicate more time to that.

It taught us that each thing we decided or did was going to have a consequence and that this consequence had to be weighed. Ultimately each person chose. That is what I would highlight.

*What was the reform like that Father Bergoglio promoted in the Society's Argentinean Province?*

That reform, obviously, Bergoglio did not accomplish alone. First, it must be understood: here, as in all of Latin America, after the Council, there arose a great increase not only in theological reflection but also in a pastoral reflection very committed to politics and social change. In Argentina, as in other countries, a movement arose whose social vision had a religious reading from the faith and our religious traditions and in which the Jesuits were much involved here in Argentina.

That vision of the social reality, marked by a religious reality, strongly marked Bergoglio's period as provincial; not only he, but also other Jesuits were affected by it. Obviously, since it was a time of crisis, strong decisions had to be made, and they caused Bergoglio's hands to tremble. He discerned a lot, consulted, and sought consensus in some things; but when he had to decide, he decided on his own account.

In general, the province (in Argentina) became accustomed to this new situation of revival and relaunching, when maybe in other parts of the Society some processes were falling down, and it was reborn with a marked orientation: a social commitment that was not marked by politics but, rather, by religion.

*What was Father Bergoglio's relationship with liberation theology?*

Here there were Jesuits like Father Scannone and theologians from the local clergy like Father Lucio Gera who proposed a non-Marxist Argentinean theology, centered on religious piety and culture. Bergoglio participated in these reflections, but his role was more one of pastoral application, as can be seen in his homilies.

*What impressed you most about Father Bergoglio as a model?*

From the beginning, it struck me that when I was in class in school, he would come in and sit down just like one of us, to listen to the entire class. Obviously he was supervising the school, because afterward he would give his observations. We all asked ourselves: Who is this man who is sitting there? With this personal and unexpected way of supervising, he made many decisions; like, for example, the decision to renovate our historic and very traditional church in Santa Fe, to recover its original beauty after the secular decoration it suffered during those years of crisis. I saw these renovation measures when I was an adolescent in school.

*What was the pastoral work of Bergoglio like as archbishop of Buenos Aires?*

He took many initiatives. With respect to the pastoral initiatives that I carry out, with people who suffer from addictions, the support he gave to work on the "periphery", the support he gave to the so-called "slum priests" is well known.

The Archdiocese of Buenos Aires is very complex, like every large city, but his presence was felt at the level of the common and ordinary person as well as by the priests who saw things changing in Buenos Aires. He especially encouraged work "at the periphery", as he says. That is also how he supported the pastoral work that he conducted in prison, with the children on the streets, in the slums. That gave the archdiocese a very strong dynamic.

*What did you experience when you saw that Cardinal Bergoglio had been elected pope?*

It was a surprise. I had supposed they were going to elect someone younger; but, well, obviously something happened. There was a lot of joy for many reasons, because of all that he has experienced, because of what his figure means, and, most importantly, because what you see with him is what he is. There's no radical difference between Jorge before and Francis after, he's the same person. Now that he is pope, he continues to be himself, and God does the rest.

*How do you think that the election of the pope, the first Jesuit, is going to influence the Society of Jesus?*

That is a very good question. It is a completely new scenario, because I do not know if Ignatius thought this would happen. Rather, I would say the opposite. Obviously, it is a message to the Society that says one has to work side by side with the pope. I believe that this is going to be an impetus toward new things, and we still do not know what they will be. Father General, in the meantime, has shown his full closeness, commitment, and support.

His election has given a great breath of fresh air and great hope to the Society. It is a confirmation for the Jesuits of many things that are being done in terms of closeness with the poorest, with those who suffer most. Obviously, as they say, you never know what a Jesuit is thinking. Therefore, it is understandable that there will be different opinions, but I believe, in the end, it is going to promote a sense of a different Church.

The Jesuit tries to be objective and critical with things, and because of that, I say that there is going to be support and rejection, but at any rate the influence of the pope's manner is going to achieve much more than his way of thinking.

*Is there some other characteristic that people should know about Pope Francis?*

I would say that Pope Francis is a person with an intellectual capacity much greater than what he shows. He is not interested in showing it, either, except when it is necessary to clarify something. He has, at the same time, the courage to propose a spiritual vision, his perspective of faith. He is a person who is capable of disconcerting for a few moments because he has a great freedom of spirit. At the same time, he seeks to listen, to seek advice, and to consult. I believe that the advisory group of cardinals has shown a lot about who he is: he can have his opinion, but he's going to seek a wider vision and, if possible, consensus.

There are going to be decisions that in due time will be very clear, not because previous popes did not make them, but I think because this pope is going to amaze us, and there are other decisions that perhaps will not be liked. Nevertheless, his hand will not tremble, this is very like him, because, I repeat, he has a lot of intellectual capacity and is more capable than is normally seen.

*Just after he was elected pope, the media accused Father Bergoglio of having collaborated with the dictatorship and of not having defended Jesuits committed to the poor ...*

These versions were spread by the media here in Argentina because there was an outbreak of fear in certain sectors that saw Bergoglio as a figure opposed to the current government, and therefore they had to discredit him. On the other hand, there were people in the same government who came out and said: "Wait a moment, let's stop, it's not like that."

In the case of Father Francisco Jalics, he himself has clarified what he wanted to say in that respect. In the case of Father Orlando Yorio, a very important Argentinean journalist who had been in the Investigative Commission on Human Rights, Magdalena Ruiz Guiñazú, explained that Yorio had told her that Bergoglio never had anything to do with his kidnapping and his illegal detention. Moreover, many said, "He saved me, he helped me, he saved other people ..."

All history has a few wounds that at the time were difficult to absorb. Bergoglio had to intervene many times in very delicate situations, and whenever someone intervenes, there is someone who does not like it, but Bergoglio was always very careful and compassionate; he helped a lot of people who were against him, people who didn't like him. This is the paradox: he has friends who don't like him or who are on a different page.

*How did Archbishop Bergoglio show his concern for life, the family, and for what our society considers the disposable?*

Bergoglio's concern for the human person I personally saw in the Society. Father Bergoglio was especially compassionate in his attention to the sick and the elderly, to the poor and to the relatives of his Jesuit brothers. At the same time, he was very stern in pointing out neglect, abandonment, or lack of charity. If he had to spend something that appeared disproportionate to help someone, he would do it wherever and however he could.

In fact, very little has been said about what Bergoglio has done in favor of the right to life, of children, especially of those exploited by the terrible scourge of human trafficking. On this matter, he presided over many public events against human trafficking and the exploitation of people, especially against prostitution, some of them in what we call "red light districts", and in these initiatives, he was supported by many non-Catholics.

*What was your experience having him as your spiritual director?*

Very diverse, because there were many years ... It is one thing when you are young and another thing when you are older. Bergoglio always sought for the person to have an encounter with God, so that in the most difficult situations or weakness, he would allow himself to be guided by what God desired. And he explained this not only with words, but with example, for he is a pious and prayerful person who always welcomed the handing over of oneself.

*Is there some story in particular that you like to remember about Father Bergoglio?*

There are many in my head, but I would like to remember when we would come to do our apostolic work, and he would challenge us to be very involved in the activities and to be with the people, to visit their houses and to get closer to their problems; we had to go back to the community at a certain time. For him, these tensions were very important because he wanted us to know how to handle the stress of apostolic responsibility by being in the community. In [the formation center at] San Miguel there is a tree-lined road that leads to the house. When you approached from afar and saw the figure in black looking at his watch, you knew he was going to tell you: "Go straight ahead because you are late" ... and as young people we would take it well, because we knew that he corrected us because it had to be done.

Many times after a lot of work, he came down with a bottle of wine and something to eat, and we ate together in order to create a family environment.

# Father Ángel Rossi, S.J.

(fifty years old, student of Father Bergoglio; now superior of the Residencia Jesuita community in Córdoba)

*How did you meet Pope Francis?*

Pope Francis, then Father Bergoglio, was provincial when I entered the Society. I do not know if you know, but for a candidate to enter the Society, he has to be admitted by the Father Provincial. He was the one who received me into the Society. Bergoglio was then very young; he was thirty-three or thirty-five years old; he was the youngest provincial in the world in the Society of Jesus. He had not been a priest for very many years; I think this already indicated a very special personality, with a lot of depth and a lot of strength.

I completed the novitiate during his term as provincial, and it was precisely he who sent me to Ecuador, together with another Jesuit, as the last act of his term in office. It was a gesture of great generosity, because it wasn't as if he told us "cheer up and go"; rather, he also offered the Father General, since his role as provincial was ending, to go to Ecuador himself.

The Father General ignored him and left him here as rector of Colegio Máximo. We left, and upon our return he was in charge of our formation during the years of studies we had left. That was the time when I had most contact with him.

*What do you remember about those years of formation?*

What I always remember about the figure of Bergoglio is that he was a spiritual man, a man of prayer. Bergoglio is a "pray-er:" a man who brings things first to prayer. Without wanting to go around measuring with a stopwatch, I would say that he prayed for at least three hours per day, and I'm sure he continues doing it because he is an early riser. When we would get up at 6:30 or 7:00 to go to Mass, Bergoglio would have already prayed and already washed the sheets and towels for 150 Jesuits in the laundry room. He would have already washed them and already hung them up when we were only just starting to get on our feet.

Secondly, I would emphasize his gentleness with people, especially his mercy. I have to say that the priest Bergoglio has a very great sense of mercy. Bergoglio is capable of forgiving what one might not be able to forgive himself. I have always said that whoever hits bottom, whoever it may be, in Bergoglio he will find shelter, and it continues to be like that today. This is true for whoever it may be, from your best friend to your worst enemy. In front of more weakness, Bergoglio works better, in a strange spiritual equation, so to speak. So if I would have to single out only one thing that always remains with me—even though I do not know if I practice it, I am nevertheless grateful for it—it is his sense of mercy. Very few times have I seen mercy at the depths to which he lives it, and it does not consist in allowing anything whatever to happen, but, rather, in taking charge of the hearts of others and suffering and enjoying life with others. And he brought this to the other person with a very refined charity, a charity of gestures. Not necessarily words; but very gently and with great sobriety, he was a tremendously concrete man at the time with his gestures. I think those who have most enjoyed his election to the pontificate are those poor people who experienced his loving care, which was great and at times at levels really heroic on his part, with gestures that were really very concrete and very great. The poorest discovered many things in him—from an ear to listen to them to complete support, such as a roof, a meal, to sitting at the foot of their bed and caring for the sick during the entire night.

I always remember going to a neighborhood, as a student, where he went to celebrate Mass on Sunday, so I met him there in his pastoral work. I remember on one occasion we arrived at the sacristy and an Italian lady was crying because they had told her that morning that her mom in Italy was extremely sick. We're talking about a very poor person, so for her it was unthinkable to travel. After Mass, we went back to Colegio Máximo to have lunch, and two hours later he called me to his room, and he gave me two roundtrip tickets and told me to "Take Asunta to the airport so that she can travel immediately."

These gestures, which might not even occur to some people, were normal for him. On another occasion, when we were making the Spiritual Exercises, on the fourth day, he called me and said to me, "You are very comfortable praying, eating, and sleeping, and at the door there is a woman with four children who does not have a roof, so leave the retreat and get her a roof over her head, and when they have a home, you can return to prayer." Just like that, you could say, he "threw me out" of the house, and that's how it was. We went back once we had completed the mission: a mission in which he intervened directly because it helped, he knew how to help, and he knew what doors to pound on for help.

*And his leadership qualities?*

Bergoglio was a very skillful man. I say that he is a mix between a desert saint and a brilliant manager, a combination that normally isn't very common.

He is a man with great intelligence, and also with academic and scholarly intelligence, but above all I think of that special perception which previously the monks used to call the cardiognosis: the gift of knowing peoples' hearts. It is an intuitive intelligence: with very little information, he knows you, he penetrates you, and you cannot hide things from him. These are people who look beyond, who have a very profound perception, who speak on a special spiritual level, with an intelligence of the heart more than of the mind, without detracting from the mind, which he has certainly developed.

I would say, therefore, that he's a mix of a man of God and a statesman, which means a man with a lot of spiritual sensitivity, but one who is able to handle fifteen important issues—from a meeting to a political issue or a great administrative decision—all at the same level and with the same effectiveness. So these are the images I have, a spiritual man, profoundly spiritual, a man of very great mercy, and a man of hands-on charity, not just in words or moans and lamentation, but lamentation that comes with hands and gestures.

*Is there some link between Bergoglio and the Manos Abiertas foundation that you direct?*

Manos Abiertas (Open Hands) is a lay foundation inspired by the strong figures of Saint Alberto Hurtado, the Chilean Jesuit saint, and Blessed Mother Teresa of Calcutta that seeks to provide concrete help, a helping hand to those who most need it.

Manos Abiertas in some way is the type of initiative that, without being directly linked to any initiative of Bergoglio, is born from the spirit he infused not only of concern for the concrete needs of people but also of not wanting to do everything oneself, of being attentive to the capacities and qualities that many other people around us have, and that's what makes this work possible.

I would say that the way the Society itself acts today would also have been impossible without what it learned from Bergoglio. Not only Manos Abiertas, but other things, too—the work of San José, the pastoral work with addictions that Father Fernando Cervera does, and many other works in Mendoza [Argentina] and in other places—carry the seal of the one who instilled in us the love of the poor, a simple way of caring for them, not from some ideology, but rather by personally loving them, being close, caring for them, and learning from them.

*What did you feel and think when you saw him come out onto the balcony of Saint Peter's . . . ?*

I was simply petrified, frozen, a mixture of immense joy and of profound surprise, considering his advanced age and certain ailments. But I see him rejuvenated, and I believe that it has fallen very well into place, because he is at ease. But certainly at the same time it is surprising and challenging to me: first, it is challenging because of his name, it challenges me religiously, and it is a challenge for me from someone who could have been setting up his retirement quarters, and suddenly in his hands he has nothing less than the entire world. He went from going around almost anonymously to being perhaps the most famous man in the world. So, these are contrasts that have been very strong, and I am surprised at his capacity to continue being himself, to manage all of this with the same simplicity and faithfulness with which he managed the parish or the Colegio Máximo kitchen.

*What impact do you think his election will have on the Society of Jesus?*

We, as Jesuits, are in faithful service to the pope; we are here for that, for what the pope orders. In this case, the pope is one of ours, so he understands our charism perfectly, and he's also going to know how to bring out the best in us. I think that the words our Father General has had with him are very confirming and consoling, loving, and completely supportive, affirming that we have to be, as indeed we should be because of our vows, totally at the disposition of the pope, who in this case is one of our brothers. Some will have to adjust their hearts because it is something novel. But what gives me confidence is knowing that few know us as he does.

# Father Enrique Eduardo Fabbri, S.J.

(ninety-two years old, professor emeritus of the Colegio Máximo San José)

*You are the oldest Jesuit in the province. How do you remember Bergoglio?*

Well, I am sixteen years older than he is. When he entered the Society, I was in Europe, and when I came back, he was studying theology here in Buenos Aires. Even though I was older than he was, we established a good friendship, with a lot of communication, despite the fact that I am a man of reflection, of investigative work, and he is a man of action. I know that my way of theological thinking troubled him a bit, but he has never been as theologically open as I am.

Nevertheless, he had this great quality of knowing how to reach people. From a young age, he could be seen to be a man born with what it takes to be a driving force, a leader.

*What was your theological difference with Bergoglio?*

I am much in line with Cardinal Martini,[1] and I agreed with him in that the Church is behind the times. I am not

[1] Carlo Maria Martini, S.J. (1927–2012) was an Italian Jesuit, rector of the Pontifical Biblical Institute, archbishop of Milan, and Cardinal of the Catholic Church. In his last interview to the Italian Press, published the day after his death, Cardinal Martini stated that the Church was "200 years behind the times."

going to say if it is two hundred years, or if it's more or less, but that we are behind in many things, on that I agreed with Martini. The schooling that the Society gave me made me very critical. I have always given some headaches; not even the Jesuits themselves can escape from a Jesuit.

Bergoglio is not a theologian with the capacity of John Paul II or Benedict XVI. I do not consider him a profound theologian. He does not have a theology degree, but he is shrewd in the exercise of what we could call the great political game.

I devote a lot of my time to preparing engaged couples and counseling marriages with moral conflicts, and that made Bergoglio a bit nervous. I have been classified as a theologian who is too advanced. And especially because I worked on a theme that is not the strongest in the Society: the whole reality of matrimonial anthropology which indicates a rather important insistence on the role that sex has in the manifestation of love. Perhaps that caused us not to have as deep a friendship as I have with others. He continued to appreciate me, but my way of thinking about marriage, about women, about sex, etc., produced a certain suspicion in him. So ultimately when we happened to meet, we would greet each other, but that was all.

I believe Bergoglio is going to push many reforms, and I am going to sit still, which is going to be a bit difficult for me.

*So you are not pleased with his election as pope . . .*

I am! God writes straight with crooked lines, and I believe that right now it is going to help the Roman Curia a lot to have a pope with the personality of Pope Francis, because he's going to teach them to be free from all that pomp, which is now worn out.

In that sense I believe it's going to be difficult for him, because the Roman Curia is strong, but he has already shown that he is courageous just in the way he assumed the role of pope. Even though intellectually we don't think alike, I believe we disagree on things that are debatable, on which I can think one way and he another. But I am convinced that for the Church this is a good that outweighs the effect his personality might have had on me as being fastidious or irritating.

I believe that in order to reach the man of today, one has to go more toward the path of the heart and not toward the path of what must be observed. That is how we win over the will. He is a very straightforward man, very simple, who gives testimony to simplicity.

*What about the versions that say that during the military dictatorship Father Bergoglio did not defend the Jesuits?*

As provincial he had many problems, but those who say there were some who were resentful toward him have exaggerated the reality because I, who did not quite understand him in everything, never felt unappreciated or a lack of support. In fact, last year, during a special event organized by the Archdiocese of Buenos Aires, I was invited and sat in the third row. Bergoglio arrived and sat in the first row. He turned around, saw me, and got up to greet me with a hug. He is like that, a man with great people skills, a gift that he's going to need a lot, I believe.

# Brother Mario Rafael Rausch, S.J.

(sixty years old and a Jesuit since 1977, friend of Pope Francis and bookbinder in Buenos Aires; his twin brother is also a Jesuit brother)

*Can you tell us what happened on March 23, 2013, just days after the election of Pope Francis?*

It was my birthday, and the pope called to wish me a happy birthday just as he's called me now for many years. He remembers our birthday, mine and that of my twin brother, because since he was the provincial, he was the one who admitted us to the Society of Jesus. With him, vocations also increased for the brothers; a vocation to being a religious brother, not a priest, is not well known in the world nowadays. He had that kind of sensibility, but he surprised me when he called me now as the pope.

*What did you talk about on this call?*

He called directly; Mrs. Raquel, the portress answered the call, and when he told her, "It's Jorge", she recognized the voice immediately and became very nervous. I was working in my bookbinding workshop, and she entered very excitedly and told me "The pope is calling!" "Well, put him through", I told her. I had hardly picked up the phone when he said to me, "Happy Birthday!" and I said to him, "How are you, Jorge? Well, Francis now." But he likes us to call him Jorge as always, and I told him, "the portress is thrilled", and he told me, "Yes, she recognized my voice."

Later he started to make some jokes, and we laughed, but I didn't want to draw the call out because I knew it was an intercontinental long-distance call, and I tried to make it short, because he always has been very austere ... I mean, very attentive, very personal, but at the same time austere.

I took advantage of the opportunity to give him my greetings and to comment that I had been speaking with one of my aunts, whom he knew, and that when I told her to pray for the pope, my aunt responded: "Yes, every time I have a difficult job, I offer it for the pope." Also, I told him that my sister sent her greetings and that she's very happy he's the new pope and so are all my brothers who called me. Everyone supposed that the pope would call me that day, and they were all right, because he called me at around 11:30 in the morning.

*What do you remember of Father Bergoglio in the days when he was provincial?*

I always admired him because he was a simple man and at the same time very happy, very spontaneous, and he joked very easily. I entered the same year he began his period as provincial. I came in August to go on a retreat given to me by another Jesuit, a priest whom he had assigned to work for vocations throughout the province, who has now passed away. Before going back to Tres Ríos with my family, I spoke with Father Jorge to ask him for admission as a brother in the Society. I spoke with him in this same house, and here was where he admitted me to the Society of Jesus. First, he told me, to see if I was scared, "Are you sure? Look, this is for your entire life." And as he saw that it didn't scare me, he laughed and told me, "Well, I gladly admit you."

Three weeks later I went back to enter the novitiate. He, as provincial, visited the novitiate every week. He visited us personally and was very close to the master of novices, whom he himself had named. While I was a novice, I remember one time he gave me a rosary that he had brought from Rome and that had been blessed by the pope. He had to travel to Rome for a month on official business, and he brought a rosary back for each novice. Besides being a man who was very close to us, he was also very demanding, very austere. He is austere with himself, first of all, and he also tried to make those he formed, the Jesuits, also continue on this path of austerity. He made it so that we would pay a lot of attention to our spiritual life and also to our apostolic life and life of service. So, I would really consider him like a father. Father, brother, friend, that is who Bergoglio is.

*You keep a letter Father Bergoglio wrote you . . . What does the letter say?*

When he finished as provincial and started to be rector of this house, I wrote him a letter as a subordinate who is grateful to his superior for his attention, his closeness, his caring, and he responded to me with this letter:

San Miguel, December 12, 1979
Reverend Brother Mario Rausch

My dear Mario:
Your letter from the eighth of this month is a letter of gratitude, and to be grateful is a virtue that Saint Ignatius wanted very much for his Jesuits to have. Knowing how to appreciate your superiors, your brothers, is a sign that you have a grateful heart for God our Lord, and a grateful heart is always a source of grace for the entire body of the Society and of the Church. Take advantage of this opportunity to thank the Lord for the many graces he has given you, for your family, your vocation, the novitiate, your piety, your virtues. Thank the Lord for

having given you the Most Holy Virgin as your Mother and Saint Joseph as a model of prayer and work. Give thanks for the virtues of each member of the community, as Saint Alphonsus Rodriguez[1] did. Finally, pray many prayers of thanksgiving, that the Lord may keep you well, with a strong embrace and all caring affection in our Lord and his Most Holy Mother,
Jorge

He was very thoughtful to answer with a letter that I had given to him hardly two days earlier, but he was like that, very thoughtful. I keep other letters that he wrote me admitting me to the various stages of formation, but this is the one I keep in a very special way.

*What surprised you most about the years when he was in charge of formation?*

That he was involved in everything, always attentive, even in the most practical things. Nothing escaped him. You could find him in the kitchen cooking, at the back of the farm and among the animals, seeing how everything was going, and you could even find him putting dirty clothes in the washing machine. He was in all things practical, but his presence was discreet, solicitous, one of service.

*What did you experience when you knew he had been elected pope?*

Well, like all the religious, when the smoke came out during the conclave, I went to the television to watch. After

---

[1] Saint Alphonsus (or Alfonso) Rodríguez, S.J. (1532–1617) was a brother doorkeeper in the Jesuit novitiate in Palma de Mallorca (Spain), where he became an example of austerity, service, and absolute obedience. He is often confused with Alphonsus (or Alfonso) Rodríguez (1526–1616), also Jesuit, the author of the classic spiritual book, *The Practice of Christian and Religious Perfection.*

the white smoke, the wait was long ... as the saying goes, he who enters the conclave as pope comes out a cardinal, according to the world; I thought to myself that if Bergoglio entered as a cardinal, there was the possibility he could come out as pope, and during this waiting time I worried a lot for him, because I felt that if he were given a great responsibility, since he was so close, I felt like it would also fall on me, and I knew that he didn't want to be pope.

Ten days before he had to travel to Rome, knowing there was going to be a conclave, I called him on the phone and asked if I could at least go to greet him, and I said to him as a joke, "because now you have to travel and you might have to stay there." He laughed and told me, "Don't worry, there's no danger." Well, he seems to have ignored the danger he was running and told me we would see each other when he returned ... so now I'm waiting for him to come to Argentina, so I can meet him.

The day of his election, some fifteen minutes before they announced the name of the new pope, I told an elderly priest in the nursing home, to tease him, "It's going to be Bergoglio", and he told me "No". Afterward, when his name was announced, the priest congratulated me, believing that I knew something, that I had said it seriously. The emotion lasted many days; I almost couldn't believe that Jorge Bergoglio, our brother, a person so close to us, to me personally, was really the pope.

*Any expectations with the new pope?*

You have to let him be. It is enough to see the good that he did, first as provincial, here in the Society of Jesus, and then, later, as director of formation, a time in which many young vocations entered the Society ... he's a man who is capable of doing a lot of good for the Church.

# Father Ignacio Pérez del Viso, S.J.

(seventy-eight years old, professor of Father Bergoglio and professor of theology in the Colegio Máximo San José in San Miguel)

*How did you meet Pope Francis?*

He entered the Society of Jesus a few years after I did, and I had him as a student in theology, which I had recently begun to teach. Let me tell you something: on one occasion, when he had an important job in the Society, we visited the apostolic nuncio together, and I said to him jokingly, "I had Father Bergoglio as a student", and Father Bergoglio immediately replied, "That's where the heresies come from, Monsignor." And the nuncio looked at us, not knowing which one of us was joking.

They made him provincial at a very young age, when he was only thirty-six years old, in July 1973. Before that, they had done a consultation of all the communities in Argentina so that they would be given names for a potential provincial, and someone from my community gave Bergoglio's name. I remember that I absolutely opposed it, saying "But he's very young, thirty-six years, don't burn him, he must be given a bit more time, he will become a good provincial. He's a good lad, a good young man." But they made him provincial at thirty-six, during a very difficult time, because in that same year we had four presidents. That same year [Juan Domingo] Perón died, and he was succeeded by his wife, who had been a dancer [Evita]. In 1976, the

45

military took control. So Bergoglio's time as provincial began during one of the most difficult periods in Argentina's history, because at the same time there were different currents among the bishops themselves: one could see that there were different positions. Some were very openly in favor of human rights. And a few, mostly military chaplains, like Bishop Bonamín, were favorable to the regime; but the majority didn't know what to do. They were dedicated to the work of the Church, to pastoral work and to helping the poor. But no one knew what was happening ... and that explains also the difficulties that Bergoglio had as provincial during that time.

*What do you remember especially from this time?*

Despite his youth, he made decisions that were necessary and appropriate. For example, we Jesuits had, at that time, three Catholic universities in Argentina, among them the university that was here [in Buenos Aires], which was called, and is still called, the Universidad del Salvador. I worked there, and it was my opinion that we were not able to continue there, and I said that we had to hand it over to a lay association. The decision was made by the Father General, but it was Bergoglio who implemented it, and in March 1975 he solemnly handed over the Universidad del Salvador to a lay association that collaborated with us, giving it the opportunity to move forward.

Well, because Bergoglio took this step, he received much criticism, since the university had to be handed over without debts. To turn it over without debts, some properties had to be sold, and because of the sale of these properties, there were also complaints. From my modest understanding, he did what was right, for the best. In other religious congregations, they have terms of office, which they complete in exactly three or four years, and they usually have the possibility of being renewed for a second term. With us, a provincial or a superior is elected for a period of around three years, and after that he can continue for a bit more. Obviously, when you are removed before those three years, it is thought that something strange was going on, unless it was to give him some new responsibility. Bergoglio was in office a total of six and a half years, from July 1973 until December 1979.

*What happened later when Father Bergoglio left his responsibility as provincial?*

He became rector of the Colegio Máximo, which includes two departments—philosophy and theology—and the place where the students live. I was there also during the six years of the following provincial. So, adding six and six, twelve long years with a great influence especially in the formation of young people.

*After that comes a period in which he was sent to Córdoba ...*

Yes, they assigned him to Córdoba, where he was for a few years. Some say he was sent as a punishment. For everyone who is from Buenos Aires, to be sent far away sounds like a punishment, but among us it's not like that. We have to tend to works throughout Argentina, and in my case, for example, Bergoglio, when he was close to finishing his term as provincial, told me, "I am going to assign you to Corrientes." I told him, "Good." There in Córdoba, he freely made himself available to give talks and retreats and to converse with anyone at all; he even wrote a book while he was there.

At the same, among us, punishment doesn't exist, which is to say, there are rebukes, but the rebukes are done in private so that the one who committed a mistake can be helped to change. In all my Jesuit life, I remember only two cases where someone was given a public rebuke through a letter from the provincial. But punishment does not go with our philosophy, because if someone wants to punish him, it's practically a way of telling him to leave.

*When he was elected pope, some accused him of having "handed over" two Jesuit priests to the military government . . .*

That's the episode of Fathers Jalics and Yorio. Yorio died in Uruguay in an automobile accident[1], and Jalics still lives in Germany and is more than eighty years old. At that time I was studying in France, but when I came back, I spoke with Bergoglio and with them, and there was undoubtedly a conflict when Bergoglio decided to take them out of the poor neighborhoods where they were working. But he wanted to take them out of there in order to save their lives.

There was a time when leaving Argentina meant saving your life. I remember Bishop Angelelli from La Rioja was killed in 1976. Many bishops had told him, "Go to Rome to take some course; leave Argentina for a while", but the bishop said, "No, the people of La Roja are going to say that I abandoned them."

The conflict occurred when the provincial told [these priests] that they should leave, and they resisted him because they said the people would feel they had abandoned them. I would not say they were being disobedient, but rather

---

[1] Father Orlando Yorio, who left the Society of Jesus, actually died from a cardiac arrest on August 9, 2000, while serving as a priest for the Archdiocese of Montevideo (Uruguay).

they raised a "conscientious objection" that at that time the Society of Jesus still had not elaborated upon in our official documents. In some later general congregation they defined the issue of the "conscientious objection" and proposed that faced with an order from a superior, a Jesuit, first, can go back to speak about it with the superior who gave it and can later appeal to Father General and also can appeal to the pope.

I believe that Jalics and Yorio raised a conscientious objection. And which of the two was right? Both were right; I mean he who gave the order and those who resisted. This happens in the Church ... maybe there is friction, clashes between different positions that cannot be harmonized, and it is a reality that causes suffering, but later there is no reason to look for the one who is guilty.

After they were arrested, Father Bergoglio tried to free them as soon as possible. It was Admiral Massera, from the Marines, who told him that the Marines knew nothing, and that was probably true, because the military had adopted a guerrilla system of independent cells.

Now, we have to bear in mind: the military easily released people officially detained, those who were in a police station or in a public prison. At times this happened to someone under house arrest, or they allowed them to leave the country, or they let them go free, but it was very uncommon for them to release somebody who had been kidnapped, because he could later become a witness, as did happen. That is why they were called "missing".

So, if the military released two who had been five months with their eyes blindfolded, tied up, and for many days not being allowed to use the bathroom ... it is because someone exerted some effective pressure. I don't see anyone else who could have put on that pressure but the Jesuit provincial, because the Jesuits still had great prestige. If not for him, I do not understand how their release could have happened.

*What other important aspects do you remember from Father Bergoglio's time in office?*

As I said, he found himself at a very difficult time, not only because of the political situation that I mentioned before, but also in the Church, because of the [Second Vatican] Council which ended in 1965. Part of the environment that remained after the Council had to do with reading the signs of the times, interpreting. Then we had meetings together in groups, and I must say that at these meetings the principle of authority was at times left aside, because what was important was for the Holy Spirit to inspire the entire group, the entire community.

And I think he saw the need to bring some order. Whenever order is put into place, that order bothers some who think differently. For example, he would ask that the students wear the clerical collar and things like that. Also, Bergoglio thought it advisable, in our faculty in San Miguel, for one professor or another not to continue teaching. Not necessarily because he was teaching heresies, but, yes because he had a different line of thought, and that also caused some criticism because some professors were suspended from teaching at San Miguel.

At the same time, he strengthened the principle of authority and took some temporary measures to make the norms stricter. Some criticized him because they thought these measures lasted too long. That is very debatable, though, because there is no mathematical formula for how long an exceptional measure should last. During this time, there were discernment meetings in every community in which the superior could come to participate. Meaning that it was a discernment process that included the superiors, but some of them were backed into corners, and it was the community that made the majority of the decisions.

*How were his years of service in the Society after being provincial?*

He was, like I said, six years as rector of the Colegio Máximo and after that in Córdoba, where he took advantage of the opportunity to spend more time writing, meditating, and also attending to people, because even when he was rector of the Colegio Máximo in San Miguel, I remember when a Jesuit who was my uncle passed away, he was with my family the entire time. He himself prepared and served coffee and tea, and the phone rang constantly, and he told me, "And, the merry-go-round starts now", meaning that the calls came in one after another.

When he finished as provincial and rector, I believe he arranged to have more time to think and to write more.

*It's in Córdoba where it was announced that he would be auxiliary bishop of Buenos Aires . . .*

Yes, in 1992. As auxiliary bishop, he was in charge of a vicariate, in Flores, one of the four into which the Archdiocese of Buenos Aires is divided. It was striking how, without having a car, he visited each one of the parishes. It came as a surprise to the pastors, but he didn't go to investigate them; rather, to be with them. For example, when he would meet one of the pastors who was a bit sick, he would tell him, "Well, get into bed, and I'll take care of the parish—he being bishop—I'll take care of it for two or three days until you feel better." The same with someone who had to make a trip, he would tell him, "Well, I'll take care of it." In fact, I saw how he won over the pastors, the priests in the vicariate where he worked as auxiliary bishop.

When he was named archbishop and created cardinal, he went more deeply into his work with the poorest of the poor. Largely, thanks to him, he changed the situation in the Church of the so-called "slum priests", who worked in the areas where the poorest and the marginalized were. For in the seventies, the slum priests lived in conflict with the bishops—the bishops hardly tolerated them, and every once in a while one was disciplined. In contrast, in the last few years—and I believe this change was brought about by Bergoglio and that he even influenced other bishops—now it's not about tolerating them but, rather, sending them and supporting them. Bergoglio himself went and walked through the streets where even the police wouldn't enter. For Bergoglio, it wasn't enough to send priests and nuns, but, rather, he would go to the streets himself. There was a famous case of a slum priest they took out of Buenos Aires and sent to Santiago del Estero because he received very serious death threats.

Well, he always worked for and with the poor, but something that did surprise me about Bergoglio was his push, as archbishop, for interreligious dialogue with Jews and Muslims. Here in Argentina something happens that happens almost nowhere else in the world, and that is that we are able to reunite the three religions. Bergoglio, as archbishop, did not limit himself just to respectful dealings with Jews and Muslims; rather, he became friends with many of them. Friendship completely changes the context.

I believe Pope Francis is going to improve the relationship with other religions significantly because he is very careful with his language and his gestures and has an important mastery of the art of communication.

*Were you pleased by his election as pope?*

Of course, it was an unforgettable moment. We were all together in a room when it was taking a long time to announce the name, and speculations started, but nobody said, "it could be Bergoglio", because we had dismissed him because of his age, and when they announced it, many couldn't believe it, they thought they had misheard it.

Right after hearing it, I withdrew to my computer; even though the emails and phone calls were pouring in, I didn't respond to anyone, and two hours later I wrote "*Habemus Francisco I*", which proposed that his election meant that Latin America can contribute to the Universal Church, for example, with the popular devotion symbolized in the Virgin of Guadalupe. It also meant that Pope Francis was going to have to put the issue of liberation theology on trial, indicating both the good parts of this theology and the aspects that must be left behind. Liberation theology has evolved; it's no longer the same as when Cardinal Ratzinger signed those documents more than twenty years ago, and Pope Francis will have to give some indications of where it can be led.

*What impact do you believe the naming of a Jesuit pope will have on the Society?*

Since this is the first time this has happened, we are all watching to see what the relationship is going to be, but the pope made the first move and called our Father General, so the relationship has started off with great cordiality.

Father General told him that just as with his predecessors, the Society of Jesus is completely at his service, for whatever he considers necessary, because many popes have entrusted special roles to the Society. For example, at the end of the Second World War, Pope Pius XII asked the Society to assume the Japanese mission in a special way, and we'll have to see if Pope Francis entrusts something special to the Society of Jesus.

# Bishop Hugo Salaberry, S.J.

(sixty-one years old, disciple of Father Bergoglio and bishop of Azul, Argentina)


*How do you know Pope Francis?*

When he was the master of novices, meaning about forty years ago, I went to do my Spiritual Exercises at the Society's novitiate. Originally, I was not going to do them with him but with a different priest who happened not to be there because of other activities, so Father Bergoglio gave them to me. From that moment, he impressed me as a very spiritual man, a man of prayer who at the same time was very active, very industrious, and efficient; and at the same time he was very respectful. It was always very easy to work with him. I knew him first as a superior, later as a co-worker, and it was always easy to work with him. Once he sees things clearly, he is very decisive.


*What was Pope Francis like as someone in charge of formation?*

I knew him when he was provincial; he admitted me into the Society; and later I knew him as rector. I would say that he encouraged formation consistent with what should be the usual Jesuit formation: If you give your word, fulfill it. If you promise someone in the neighborhood that you are going to see him, go and see him. Don't say yes and afterward don't go. If you have to be somewhere at a certain time, fulfill it. These are basic Jesuit issues.

The more universal a good is, the more people you reach, the more divine it is ... Charity is done in works, not so much in words. These are things from Saint Ignatius, and he tried to convey them clearly through formation. I say, very lovingly, that they were the "obsessions" of Saint Ignatius, which have not yet been fully implemented in our life, that is what he promoted. So, he encouraged the strong trend in the Society for human development. Human development from a very strong spirituality: from the spiritual dimension to everything else, whether political, social, or economic.

*Some of his critics link him [Bergoglio] with the military dictatorship ...*

No, under no circumstances. This issue has been completely clarified by the judgment issued by two people with a lot of authority here in Argentina: Professor Fernández Meijide, an ex-minister from the De la Rua Government and a politician with a long track record who has studied the issue extensively, and later Adolfo Pérez Esquivel, Nobel Peace Prize winner during that time, who gave a clear judgment about his non-collaboration. From everything they have studied, nothing appears anywhere that had anything to do with the dictatorship.

I can assure, on my part, that he in fact had no relationship and no sympathy; on the contrary, I believe he helped a lot of people. Those who did not live during this time don't know, they have no idea of the problems that we who worked in the social sphere had. I have always worked in the social sector, and there were episodes and events that are not necessary to describe, but I can say that he and the Society backed our country during those very difficult years when such atrocious injustices were committed.

*Some of the pope's first gestures don't surprise those who know him . . .*

Yes, many gestures that have surprised the world, for those who truly know him, are ordinary things that Father Jorge has always done. Of course, for those who don't know him, those gestures are very novel or perhaps uncommon at this level of the Church, but it is good that people know that. In this sense, it does us good to know he is a simple person with common tastes. At the same time, he's a pope who is in continuity with his predecessors. We always take, as bishops, the directives that come to us from the pope, whoever it may be, but each pope has a personality, a distinctive tone that serves as an example and stimulus. One desires to have a closeness to the people, like John Paul II, or exceptional conceptual clarity, like Benedict XVI, or the capacity to express ideas as Paul VI expressed them. In short, I believe that in our time, we have had some very good popes, each one of whom has had a particular tone that has served us as a paradigm for Catholics.

*What did you think when you saw him named pope?*

We Jesuits learn that the mission always comes with carrying the cross. Missions are always well received, but joy cannot be overwhelming precisely because of the weight of the cross. I celebrated his nomination with joy, but as someone who has walked close to him, we have accompanied him in this new moment with a different attitude. As I wrote in a letter to my faithful in the diocese: we can say that we have walked with him through Galilee and Samaria and Judea, now he has arrived at the moment of his ascent to Calvary. So, we will accompany him as we have accompanied him in other circumstances.

Pope Francis has always taught that if one wants to be a disciple of the Lord, he must know that we are en route with him to Jerusalem, not in some fatalistic or fortuitous or bitter way. This is the destiny accepted by those who are called. So, looking at it like this, a mission is celebrated, but euphoria is a bit out of place. This is very Jesuit.

I emphasize this only to make clear that the naming of Pope Francis is very different from what the world thinks in general: "If he has this responsibility, great! What a career he has had! How far he has gone!"... When in reality our definition of "career" is that he who most wants to advance knows he must lower himself.

*What gifts does Pope Francis bring, as a Jesuit, to the Church?*

Before all else, what I have already indicated, he is a man of prayer, of the Church, very clear in making decisions and carrying them out to the end. He's also a very effective man, because he prioritizes well and does not give importance to secondary things. Instead, he emphasizes concern for people, for the person. Bergoglio has never had an abstract concern; he always is concerned about the concrete person, the victim of injustices or poverty. As a priest and a bishop, he went through many neighborhoods in Buenos Aires where he always knew people by name, and, because of this, people love him a lot.

*What impact do you think the pope is going to have on the Society of Jesus?*

The pope is properly the superior of the Society, because we have a vow of fidelity to the pope, so he is now our superior, and he has met cordially with Father General, Father Adolfo Nicolás Pachón ... So, I think he's going to give us new missionary momentum, as the Society has always had, but now with a Jesuit pope.

*Do you see some special value in the fact that the pope is Argentinean, from Latin America?*

Right now, there is an impression of Argentineans that comes perhaps from some who emigrate from here or who are tourists abroad, and in reality our people have more characteristics in common with Bergoglio than with those who travel abroad and give the impression that most have of Argentineans.

Latin America, on the one hand, is a very similar, united reality, and with a shared identity. If a pope had come from another one of our countries, we would have celebrated as well. His election, by the design of Providence, has encouraged us, or brought consolation, to use a spiritual term. That brings encouragement interiorly and, in the world, a commitment to our Church and a greater fervor. We have seen that very clearly, for example, in the way—for instance—many people in our countries have come closer to the churches. I hope that this encouragement to live the faith grows and lasts; I desire it with my whole heart.

# Father Juan Carlos Scannone, S.J.

(eighty-one years old, professor of Jorge Mario Bergoglio)

*The pope sent you a letter a little while ago ...*

Yes, I received a letter from Pope Francis because of the interview I gave to *L'Osservatore Romano* about him. But that was before he had sent me an email because I form part of the Red Latinoamericana de Pensamiento Social de la Iglesia [Red LAPSI], which has members from Mexico to Chile and Argentina, including Brazil and the Caribbean.

When the cardinals were gathered in Rome before the conclave, the idea came up to send them what we in our network hoped for in a new pope. All of us drafted the letter and we sent it to the cardinals. I sent it to various cardinals, including Cardinal Bergoglio, who was already in Rome.

Everything indicates that the letter reached him after he was already pope, through someone who went from Argentina, probably one of the auxiliary bishops, because in his email to me he says: "Thank you for the message that was brought to me from Buenos Aires."

That was almost immediately after he was elected pontiff. Later, a thank you letter arrived for the interview I gave to *L'Osservatore*, where he wrote that "you said all the good things [about me] and left out the bad" ... very simple and very cordial, as always.

*How did you meet Pope Francis?*

I have known him for many years because he was a student of mine in the seminary of the Archdiocese of Buenos Aires. Before becoming a Jesuit, he thought of being a diocesan priest and first entered the seminary. He had already completed his secondary education, but he had not studied Latin because secondary education in Argentina does not include classical humanities. I was at that time, what we call a "regent": between philosophy and theology, we Jesuits spend some time teaching in a school or in a similar apostolate, and as I had a degree in philosophy, I went to teach at the minor seminary of the Archdiocese of Buenos Aires, which at that time we Jesuits directed; some years later it passed to the clergy of the archdiocese.

I taught high school classics, where I also had as a student Cardinal Sandri,[1] though he was among the adolescents. There was a section of the minor seminary where there were the so-called "Latinists", those who had enough studies to be able to enter the university—and some of them had a university degree and wanted to be priests, but they had to study Latin and the classics for two years. Bergoglio was my student in Greek and in literature, so that is how I met him. After finishing those two years, instead of going on to the major seminary to study philosophy, he entered the Jesuit novitiate in Córdoba. Later, he studied eight years in Europe, and between our studies we have what we call the third probation, which is a year like a new novitiate, after the priesthood. When I returned at the end of 1967, he was studying theology here [at the Colegio Máximo de San José, in San Miguel, in the province of Buenos Aires], because in his case he had three years of

---

[1] Born in Buenos Aires (Argentina) in 1943, Cardinal Leonardo Sandri is the prefect of the Congregation for the Oriental Churches in the Vatican.

philosophy and four years of theology. Between the two, it was his turn to also do his "regency".

During that time of formation, I saw him again. I remember having gone to his first Mass, where I ran into a cousin of mine. I found out there that she had been Bergoglio's first-grade teacher and that he visited her, and continued to visit her even later as bishop. This cousin of mine died when she was almost one hundred years old, well past ninety, and Bergoglio, being bishop, had continued to visit her.

When he finished theology, he was ordained a priest. He did his third probation in Spain and went back to being a master of novices for more than two years. I remember it well because I liked him a lot; even though he was five years younger than I, I was well in tune with him spiritually. Later, they made him provincial, and he moved the Curia here where we lived together for many years, and later as rector we continued to live together here, in this house. So I figure he lived in this house some seventeen years, adding up the different periods.

*What is the position of the Pope Francis today with respect to liberation theology?*

There are different currents in liberation theology, and one of them is the Argentinean current. I have written a lot about liberation theology, and one of my works later helped the cardinal, who at that time was not cardinal, Bishop Quarracino,[2] who was archbishop before Bergoglio, when

---

[2] Cardinal Antonio Quarracino (1923–1998), born in Salerno, Italy, immigrated as a child to Argentina where he was a priest, bishop, and finally archbishop of Buenos Aires from 1990 to 1998. Cardinal Quarracino is credited with having requested the then Father Bergoglio as auxiliary bishop of Buenos Aires and later as coadjutor archbishop. Cardinal Bergoglio succeeded him in the administration of the Archdiocese of Buenos Aires and as Primate of Argentina.

he was the secretary of CELAM [the Latin American Episcopal Council]. Cardinal Quarracino presented, in *L'Osservatore Romano*, the first document of the Congregation for the Doctrine of the Faith on liberation theology, and he distinguished between four currents, quoting—without naming it—the article I had written two years earlier.

There is an Argentinean current, which Gustavo Gutiérrez himself says is a current with its own characteristics of liberation theology, which never used Marxist categories or the Marxist analysis of society, but which, without disregarding the social analysis, prefers a more historical-cultural analysis.

In Argentinean liberation theology, Marxist social analysis is not used but, rather, a historical-cultural analysis not based on class warfare as a determining principle for the interpretation of society and history. I think Bergoglio's pastoral work is understood in this context. My opinion is that the Argentinean line of liberation theology, which some call "theology of the people", helps in understanding the pastoral work of Bergoglio as bishop, just as many of his affirmations and teachings do. In fact, during the time of the military government, I wrote several articles along these lines about liberation theology. Furthermore, when he was master of novices, he supported my going to the Escorial, to an event for the introduction of liberation theology in Europe.

I was going to go as a regular participant, but in the middle I was called to take charge of an issue and a seminar, something that changed my life, because it brought me to an international level.

I was very critical, above all, of the theology that Hugo Assmann[3] had presented and of the indiscriminate use of

[3] Hugo Assmann (1933–2008), Brazilian theologian considered to be one of the pioneers of liberation theology in Latin America. Assmann proposed the incorporation of Marxism into theological analysis. During the 1980s, he

Marxist analysis that Assmann made, and this was exactly what I explained at the Escorial. I had a seminar where I used texts from Juan Luis Segundo[4] and from Gustavo Gutiérrez[5] about God, and I met, among others, Pedro Trigo, who afterward also became an important liberation theologian.

Bergoglio supported me along these lines. I don't know that he agreed with me 100 percent, but he read my work and even supported me. During the time of the military government in Argentina, since I could have been censured, he advised me, when he was the provincial, to send my articles—for example, I remember that one came out in *Christus*, from Mexico, about the theory-praxis relationship in liberation theology—not to send them from the post office in San Miguel because they could have been censored, but rather to send them from some post office in Buenos Aires. In such a way, he always supported me; moreover, when they asked him about my doctrine, for example Cardinal [Juan Carlos] Aramburu in Buenos Aires or Cardinal [Raúl] Primatesta in Córdoba, he always said that it was completely orthodox.

---

left the priesthood, founded the Ecumenical Association of Theologians from the Third World, and ended his career as professor in the Universidade Metodista de Piracicaba (Brazil).

[4] Father Juan Luis Segundo, S.J. (1925–1996) was born in Montevideo, Uruguay and was formed as a Jesuit in Argentina. He was one of the most important figures of liberation theology in Latin America.

[5] Gustavo Gutiérrez Merino, was born in Lima, Peru in 1928. He is one of the most published and prolific theologians of liberation theology, especially since the publication of his book, *A Theology of Liberation: History, Politics, Salvation* (1971), one of the most translated theological books of the twentieth century. In 1987, Father Guitérrez's book was the subject of an investigation by the Congregation for the Doctrine of the Faith, presided over by the then Cardinal Joseph Ratzinger, who carried out a process of modifications to his writings, the first of which was a new introduction entitled, "Expanding the View", to the second edition of *A Theology of Liberation* (1988).

Later, when he was rector, he organized a congress [1985], and I helped in the organization on an academic level. It was held here on theology about the evangelization of culture and the inculturation of the Gospel. This was one of the first events of this type to be held in Latin America, on a public level, about inculturation. On the evangelization of culture there had been a lot, but not about inculturation, an issue that was very important in [the Third General Conference of the Latin American Episcopate of] Puebla [Mexico]. For, without using the word, there was talk of the incarnation of the Gospel in popular Latin American Catholicism. Above all, there was a theologian, Lucio Gera, who was little known because he had written very little, who was a professor of theology in the theology department in the seminary of the archdiocese and who was the principal promoter of this theological current.

When I participated in the congress about Latin American theology held last year in San Leopoldo [Brazil], the image of Lucio Gera appeared there again among the dead. When Gera died, Cardinal Bergoglio buried him in the cathedral as a special courtesy, with a plaque that says he was an expert on the Second Vatican Council and the documents of [the Second Latin American General Conference of the Latin American Episcopate] Medellín and Puebla.

There was another theologian who died a while back, Rafael Tello. Cardinal Aramburu had always supported Gera, but there were problems with Tello, and for a time he was suspended "a divinis". When a priest wrote a book about Tello, compiling his unpublished texts, Cardinal Bergoglio, as archbishop of Buenos Aires, participated in the presentation of the book and vindicated him, saying: there was a time when the hierarchy had problems with him; now the hierarchy comes here to present his book.

There are things that I believe distinguished Bergoglio in a special way, above all the issue of the evangelization of culture, an issue of popular piety. One thing that is very like Bergoglio is to speak of the faithful people. When he came out onto balcony [of Saint Peter's, when he was elected pope], the first thing he did was to ask the faithful to pray for him so that God would bless him, before he gave the blessing to the people. That is very much like him.

He always supports this type of theology, and I believe that formed part of the environment where he did his pastoral work. In fact, the issue of popular piety and the evangelization of culture and the inculturation of the Gospel are key to this line of theology.

Both CELAM and the Congregation for the Doctrine of the Faith recognized the importance of this Argentinean theology for the culture, for popular piety. Bergoglio gives a lot of importance to the faithful people. It was because of this that his first reaction in front of the people gathered in Saint Peter's Square was this [asking them to pray for him] and, secondly, to show himself as bishop of Rome, creating a collegial moment with all the other bishops.

*How do you interpret his first gestures as pope?*

The night of his election, he said, "Tomorrow I am going to pray to the Virgin." I said, I am sure he is going to go to Santa Maria Maggiore, to the *Salus populi romani*,[6]

---

[6] "Protector of the Roman People" is the name that is given to the Byzantine icon of the Virgin and the Child that is found in the Roman Basilica Santa Maria Maggiore.

and I said it in an interview with *L'Osservatore Romano.* Why? I explained to them that before becoming archbishop, he was the auxiliary bishop, vicar of an area in Buenos Aires that is called Flores, which is where he was born. Once I had to give a retreat to some Dominican Sisters who live in the same block where the vicariate of Flores is located, where there is also a retirement home for elderly priests. In those days I slept in the parish rectory, which is between the vicariate and the retirement home for elderly priests. I went to greet the Vicar of Flores, and he mentioned that I was going to Rome, because I had been giving classes for ten years as a visiting professor at the Pontifical Gregorian University. He told me, now that you are going to Rome, go by Santa Maria Maggiore and bring me a prayer card from the *Salus populi romani,* which means he had a devotion to this image of the Virgin before he became pope. He not only encourages popular piety, it is obviously something very important to his pastoral work and theology, and he also participates in this piety, he lives it.

Another anecdote. After his time as provincial and rector, he went for a few months to Germany to get a doctorate, which he did not finish, about Romano Guardini, because he has a lot of regard for Guardini's theology, above all the classic theme that has been translated [into Spanish] as *contrasteidad,* but this is not a Spanish word, which would be *contrariedad* (opposition), but German: *Gegensatz.* Guardini has a dialectic that is neither Hegelian nor Marxist, a form of dialectic of opposites, in German *Gegensatz,* and in the plural, *Gegensätze.* This perspective is presented by Guardini in a book that is called *Der Gegensatz,* which I have been told has been translated into Spanish as *Contrasteidad,* where the elements are in a living tension and are never resolved into a synthesis, as some interpret Hegel.

He went to study in Munich, where Romano Guardini's archives are. An hour away from Munich by train is Augsburg. There is a very beautiful Virgin that I went to see as a work of art when I was studying for my doctorate in Munich: it is the Virgin Mary, Undoer of Knots. He brought the Virgin Mary, Undoer of Knots, from there, and with the passing of time, especially in the last few years, a very special devotion to the Virgin Mary, Undoer of Knots, has grown here. The image shows the Immaculate Mary untying knots from a white ribbon she is receiving from an angel, while another angel receives what has already been untied. A very strong devotion has been created all over Buenos Aires. In Buenos Aires, in the church of San José del Talar, there is the image just like the one in Augsburg, to which the people have a lot of devotion. The pastor here in San Miguel, where there is a similar image, by the Jesuit Merediz, told me recently: I have been able to reach the youth through youth groups, educate a group of parish schools and parishes, get vocations for the Jesuits as well as for the diocese and other religious congregations, etc., but I have never been able to reach people who never go to Mass. It was through Mary, Undoer of Knots, for whom on the eighth day of each month we have a pilgrimage; and long lines emerged to pray this devotion to the Virgin, with conversions, confessions of people who had not confessed for thirty or forty years. That is to say, it is a sociological phenomenon, but, more than anything, a spiritual and pastoral phenomenon. For someone who is a believer, the grace of God is working, and it was Bergoglio who brought her from Germany. People have gone from Argentina to Germany, and I have also. When I went to Germany, from train to train, I got off at Augsburg to visit the Virgin. I had seen it many years before as a work of art and now as a devotion.

A professor told me that when she went to Augsburg and bought prayer cards of the Virgin to give out, people said there that "the crazy Argentineans come here to buy hundreds of prayer cards and things", because in Germany they do not pay much attention to it.

*What impact might this have on his pontificate?*

What is interesting is that the priest is now pope who brought this devotion that has done much good and through which many people have come back to the Church. I believe that at this moment, it has a very large symbolic value: to untie the knots.

There are so many knots in our lives, and I myself see this, because every Sunday I go to hear confessions at the parish. Knots that are psychological, economic, spiritual, family, etc. This issue seems very important to me because I have not seen anything said about it. So many things are being said about the pope, but I do not think much has been said about this devotion up until now. I think it is a very interesting topic; it gives theological and pastoral value to popular piety and the inculturation of the Gospel. Obviously, it is different in every country, but there is always something in common—especially Marian devotion.

I think this helps us to understand the importance Bergoglio gives to the people, and above all to the faithful people and even more to the poor, because it is united to the preferential option for the poor. He, as archbishop of Buenos Aires, supported what we call the "slum priests" a lot. The slum priests considered him one of them because he supported them so much. Father Carlos Galli, who was with me in that LAPSI network, shared something that is key for understanding Bergoglio.

Bergoglio went to [the Fifth General Conference of the Latin American Episcopate in] Aparecida [Brazil] and had a very important role there. He was also the substitute relator, but as the principal relator had to leave, he, in fact, was the relator to a great extent, and later directed the drafting commission, where Father Galli helped as well. Before going to Aparecida, Galli asked him what were the most important things that had of necessity to be treated at Aparecida. He told him: "Christ and the poor." Christ and the poor, as they give the key to understanding. Aparecida speaks of pastoral conversion, of outdated structures that must be overcome, and of the Church that must be in a state of mission.

Before going to Rome, he left a document I liked so much I made a copy of it even though I was not from his diocese. It was directed to priests, pastors, and to the directors of educational institutions of the Archdiocese of Buenos Aires and exhorts them to go out to the street. Meaning, it is not enough to wait in churches for people to come; rather, we have to go out and preach the Gospel. I believe that the name Francis goes beyond poverty, which is the most important. What Francis did was that he reformed the Church with his friars. Francis—Saint Francis of Assisi—preached on the streets. Archbishop Bergoglio, for example, had a huge tent put in the Constitution Plaza, which is a huge plaza that is next to the southern train station, where priests attended to the people passing by, who asked for everything from the blessing of a prayer card to spiritual direction or confession. Meaning, they went out to the streets, there, in the plaza. That is to say, to seek those who are away. It is a bit like what the pastor here was saying about the Virgin, the Undoer of Knots, there are people who do not go to Mass but who go in the procession on the eighth day.

*Is there is another theme you consider to be important in Pope Francis' life?*

Another aspect that I believe is going to be very important for him now, as pope, is dialogue with Jews and Muslims. He has many very good friends who are Rabbis and who are from different orientations within Judaism, even politically speaking. The same is true of Islam. This is one of the few places in the world, I believe, where there has been dialogue between Jews and Muslims, thanks to the mediation of the Catholic Church. This is what he has achieved in Buenos Aires. Ecumenism, but above all interreligious dialogue. That is very notable, and I believe he is going to implement it as pope.

*What is his vision of America as a continent?*

Bergoglio greatly esteemed Alberto Methol Ferré, a lay Uruguayan who is also a very good friend of mine, from the magazine *Vísperas*, which the Uruguayan dictator shut down. When he was archbishop, Bergoglio gave many priests a book by Methol Ferré that stressed the unity of Latin America and the theme of the "Great Homeland" from a Catholic viewpoint.

Methos, who was a friend of mine also, was a lay theologian, historian, and philosopher, all self-taught, because he did not have a university degree. He was a big supporter of the unity of Latin America, not only on a cultural level, which it has, but also on an economic and political level. Bergoglio gave his book to people. He also appreciated another Uruguayan, Guzmán Carriquiry,[7] who is now in

---

[7] Professor Guzmán Carriquiri, layman, is the secretary of the Pontifical Commission for Latin America in the Vatican.

Rome and for whom he wrote the prologue to one of his books.

*Can you explain a bit more about the concept of the "faithful people" for the pope?*

Well, the concept of the "faithful people", as I said, is very Bergoglio, and he used it frequently as Jesuit provincial and as bishop. It is the People of God, the simple people. This theme and its importance emerged in the Episcopal Pastoral Commission, which was led by Lucio Gera. When the commission was dissolved, we continued meeting and working together with Bishop Joaquín Sucunza, current Vicar General of Buenos Aires. Methol Ferré also came to these meetings from Uruguay.

We reflected on the importance of the People of God, above all the poor, to conserve popular religiosity, popular piety, and popular culture. So, the faithful people are the People of God, believers, the simple and those whose core is the poor, the excluded, and, I believe Bergoglio himself invented the word, the "disposables".

These are faithful people who not only believe but also evangelize, through popular religiosity, through—many times—grandmothers and mothers, who teach their children the desire to pray. This theme is proper to the Argentinean theology that influenced Bergoglio, at least on a pastoral level. It is because of this that he proposed it in Aparecida, together with that very important process of pastoral conversion—of going out into the street—that was very typical of his pastoral work. It's not only about the religious moment, but also about the social one: the fight against injustice and against its causes, even the structural ones.

*How did you receive the news that Cardinal Bergoglio had been elected pope?*

In the beginning I could not believe it, since I thought that because of his age they were not going to elect him. He was already seventy-six years old, and he had already resigned, even though they had not yet accepted his resignation as archbishop. I did not expect it. I was very pleased, but what most pleased me was when he came out onto the balcony and started to give those incredible signals, perceived by the entire world. He made an impact even on non-Catholics, which is incredible and thanks to small gestures: not putting on the red cape, not using the golden cross but, rather, an ordinary one that he had as bishop, keeping the coat of arms he had as bishop with the typical IHS from the Society of Jesus, calling himself Francis, not living in the Papal Apartments.

The letter I received, handwritten, says, "F. Casa Santa Marta", the postal number, Vatican City. With only the letter "F", who was going to say that it was Pope Francis! Handwritten, even on the envelope. He telephoned, for example, my [Jesuit] brother Mario Rausch on his birthday. He says that he always calls him, but of course, it was one thing when he was Father Bergoglio, another thing when he was Bishop or Cardinal Bergoglio, but quite another thing when he became pope, and he called them, him and his twin brother, both of them. And so, with the simplicity and austerity of a deeply spiritual man.

Together with this simplicity and profound spiritual life, there is another aspect. He will not be afraid to make changes, and this has been the case since he came out onto the balcony. For some people, this has fallen on them like a blow to the body, these very simple attitudes. He, indeed, is an austere and simple spiritual man, but at the same time, if he sees that something has to be done for the good of the Church, he's going to do it. He knows how to move around, to be diplomatic, he has Italian blood, and because of that I say that what he has to do, he will do it without a doubt and without shaking his fist, but trying to avoid collisions wherever possible. I say, where possible, because he is going to collide with many if he changes the things that need to be changed. The naming of an international commission of cardinals to study the reforms of the Curia, the naming of a Franciscan for the first vacant position in the Curia, as Secretary for the Congregation for Institutes of Consecrated Life and Societies of Apostolic Life, I think marks a notable advance even with symbolic gestures, so much can be hoped for. He always says "pray for me", and he told me that in a letter. I responded to him that I pray a lot for him, because—for me, and I firmly believe this—this is a very special moment for the life of the world and of the Church. I believe that Divine Providence has prepared him a place where he can do a lot of good for the Church and for the world.

# Father Enrique Laje, S.J.

(eighty-five years old, Jesuit since 1944, professor of Jorge
Mario Bergoglio)

*Tell us how you met Pope Bergoglio.*

I came from Chile, where I studied languages, to take on the
responsibility of the philosophy students of our formation center in San Miguel. There he was my student, a good student,
diligent, active, and one who helped in community things.
He was even the proctor of the philosophy students, and I
had daily contact with him. There I saw he had a great capacity for work, very good people skills, and he was very help-
ful. I went to Europe to continue my formation, and upon
returning I had him again when he was starting his theological studies at the Colegio Máximo San José. He was my student in first year theology in ecclesiology and the social
doctrine of the Church; he also worked with me when I
was in charge of the library. He was really my right-hand
man, especially with editing the internal magazine and editing books. Later he was ordered back to Colegio Máximo as
rector, so I had him for many years as superior and later as
provincial. So I had contact with him during different stages
of his life as a student, as a priest, and later as a superior.

*What do you remember about Father Bergoglio as provincial of
Argentina?*

He was a very efficient and very active man. He encoun-
tered a very difficult situation in the Universidad del Salvador,

which had a very large debt. He arranged to refinance it and later handed over the university to the council of laymen, since there were not enough Jesuits to maintain three universities. Later, internally he had to put things in order. When he brought order to all that disorder, it is only logical that some would suffer a bit in the reorganization and that some antipathy would result from it. The same thing that is going to happen in Rome when he puts in order some things in the Curia that are said not to be going well, because he is very much an executive.

*How did Pope Bergoglio see the issue of liberation theology?*

He adopted a position of maintaining dialogue with everyone without getting involved in the issue. I remember that I wrote a very tough article on liberation theology that was published in the magazine *Stromata* and that caused a lot of dissatisfaction among those who were along those lines. They went to him and complained, because he was the provincial, for having allowed me to write the article. He responded to them: "Well, if you do not agree, write something to refute it, if you can." In the article, I make evident that the use of Marxist analysis in liberation theology leads to the choice of class warfare and other errors; and above all it leads to the fundamental ambiguity of confusing faith as a response to God who reveals himself in Christ with the commitment to impose socialism.

*Some say that his time in Córdoba, and later as rector of Colegio Máximo, was a punishment . . .*

He was in Córdoba a short time, because soon after being sent he was named auxiliary bishop by Cardinal Quarracino. I saw him there because I had gone to Córdoba to teach some courses on Catholic culture. There I remember he dedicated a lot of time to the confessional and pastoral things. The idea that he was being punished there is debatable.

*What stands out during his time as archbishop of Buenos Aires?*

As archbishop of Buenos Aires, he maintained a low profile, living a very austere life and not wanting to live in the archbishop's palace. Instead, he lived in a room in the Curia. He made his own dinner, went to the supermarket, traveled by bus, traveled by subway, he did not go by car or with a driver, but he united his austerity to many works of mercy, because he visited the sick, he visited the poor.

Of course he had his moments of conflict with the government because the cardinal, in a homily for the anniversary of the homeland, made some criticisms that were applied to all Argentineans, and that was not appreciated. But whenever he spoke about controversial national issues, he did so based on fact and from a moral point of view, not from that of party politics. But it still caused irritation because some thought that nothing can be said about the Gospel that has anything to do with reality. That is not true. There are, of course, certain things that are incompatible with Christian morality.

He also entered into conflict by defending issues like the right to life of the unborn and the unique nature of marriage between a man and a woman. He defended this when the minister of health was an abortionist. The Church is always going to criticize this because she is in favor of life, in favor of the Gospel and of moral and natural law.

In this, the cardinal did nothing more than be Catholic. All serious Catholics are going to be in favor of life. Even the Argentinean Constitution recognizes that life starts from conception, and if I have a human life, I am a human person and have the right to life.

*Pope Francis also has had an important concern for the elderly . . .*

He always had something that is very evangelical, and that is concern for the weak, in the sense—on the one hand, the child and, on the other hand, the elderly. At the beginning of life, the human person is extremely weak and needs special care; and the same when a person is arriving at the end of life. Specifically, with respect to the elderly, Cardinal Bergoglio always emphasized the respect they deserve as people with experience and wisdom who, because of their experience, in every culture, have an advisory role.

*What did you feel when they elected Bergoglio as pope?*

First, I was surprised, because among the first news reports that came, it was said that the cardinals were seeking a pope who was between sixty and seventy years old. The day he was elected I was eating lunch, and I had turned on the radio to a news station, and just then they were saying that the election of the cardinals could bring a surprise . . . and at three in the afternoon they announced that it was Bergoglio. It surprised me very much at first, because I did not even expect this news to come, and afterward it turned into a joy for the entire world. For the first time, we have a non-European, American, Argentinean, and Jesuit pope.

*How do you think Pope Francis is going to face the issue of liberation theology?*

I do not know if he is going to give it much importance, because liberation theology was a bit trendy, and that is over, even though the issue of the marginalized and the "option" for the poor remains unsettled; that has evolved into the term "preferential love", because to opt means to choose some and exclude others, and the Church does not exclude anyone.

*What impact can the election of a Jesuit pope have on the Society of Jesus?*

The Society of Jesus because of its nature is always linked to the pope. I believe that now this link is going to be easier, first of all because the pope is Jesuit and Father General is Spanish, and that facilitates dialogue. Pope Francis, at the same time, has a way of doing things that is very free, very personal. He himself took the initiative to call Father General, and there is the anecdote where he asks the secretary if they are praying for him to "go backward or to go forward". That is typical of him; he has a good sense of humor, but he also constantly asks for prayers because he is conscious of his responsibility.

# Father Fernando Albistur, S.J.

(professor of biblical studies at the Colegio Máximo San José, student of Father Bergoglio)

*What was most remarkable about having Father Bergoglio as a professor?*

Pope Francis is without a doubt a man of God, a person given over to God. He has always lived his following of Jesus as a Jesuit in a profound way, and we always saw the traits of the spirituality of Saint Ignatius and the Society of Jesus that have marked him very deeply. As Saint Ignatius of Loyola put at the end of his Spiritual Exercises, the motto of a Jesuit's life is complete love and service of God. Pope Francis, before and after being bishop, has lived that spirituality of service, of apostolic work dedicated to God. He is a person with an enormous capacity to work and to do many things at the same time; sometimes we saw him writing a spiritual article while putting clothes in the washing machine so that later, during the break, the students could pick up their sheets and towels. He could also be busy in the kitchen or attending people, always living the Jesuit spirituality. Here I believe we have to remember the figure of the great spiritual master in the Society of Jesus, Father Miguel Ángel Fiorito. Father Fiorito, who was a philosophy professor in this faculty, completely dedicated himself to Ignatian spirituality and was like a great spiritual master for an entire generation.

Father Francis met with Father Fiorito in 1961 when he came as a philosophy student. That year, Father Fiorito would have been forty-five years old and was a professor and director of formation. He took him as his spiritual master and there deepened his spirituality as a Jesuit, bringing out his own characteristics, which in the first place had to do with the union between the prayer and action, the prayer and work of Saint Ignatius; to be contemplative also in action, meaning, the Jesuit encounters God in apostolic work, with people, and in service. He also learned something important for us, discernment. To discern is to encounter the will of God, to encounter the way, to encounter what will give the greatest glory to God, the greatest good possible. Pope Francis has always lived that, and he insisted upon it during our formation, that we search out what more we are able to do, a little bit more, wherever possible.

Spiritual discernment is, well, one of the great dimensions of Pope Francis, learned in great part from Father Fiorito in this house. This stretching for what is more carries with it something very Jesuit, which is the apostolate on the frontiers. If you read the writings of Father Jorge, today Pope Francis, you will always see this concern to go to the frontiers, and not only geographic frontiers, but rather the frontiers of poverty, of exclusion, and of those who are farthest away from God, and also spiritual frontiers.

*This would have influenced his leadership as provincial ...*

Well, it is very telling that when he was named superior of the Jesuits in Argentina in 1973, almost immediately afterward he started to send Jesuits as missionaries into rural areas.

He continued our missions in the Rioja, soon after we retook the mission in San José del Boquerón, in Santiago del Estero, where we Jesuits had been since the end of the 1700s, a place of extreme poverty where the people were absolutely helpless. That shows his desire to go to the frontiers, to go to those who are the farthest away, to the excluded, to the poorest of the poor. In 1985, when Pope Francis was superior of this house, we celebrated the four hundredth anniversary of the arrival of the Jesuits in Argentina. To celebrate it, he decided to do two things, an international theological congress on the evangelization of culture and the inculturation of the Gospel; and at the same time a parish mission.

We were having theologians come from Europe, America, India, China, Japan, while at the same time we were also doing missions in poor neighborhoods and the parish we have here at Colegio Máximo. Both things are important, both things are on the frontier, to think about theology but also to reach those who are farthest away, the humble, the most excluded. In the Church, this spirit is summed up in the washing of feet in the Gospel according to Saint John. It is a gesture we celebrate during the evening Mass on Holy Thursday and is one to which Pope Francis always gave great importance as a priest and as archbishop of Buenos Aires. This gesture of love and humility, out of love, putting oneself at the service of the disciples by washing their feet, Pope Francis repeated it as archbishop of Buenos Aires, going to the poorest of the poor and going to the people with the greatest suffering. For example, one year he did it in the Hogar de San José, a house we Jesuits have in Buenos Aires for people who live on the street. Another year, it was in the maternity ward of a poor district of Buenos Aires where people go from the poorest neighborhoods; he did it in the Muñiz hospital, where they attend people with infectious diseases and which is currently the center for people infected by AIDS. It must have surprised many people that the pope went to prison to wash feet, but that was the sort of thing he usually did as archbishop of Buenos Aires.

*How did Father Jorge convey the Jesuit identity?*

In my personal case, and in the case of many others from my time, I would say that he helped us himself. He is a natural leader, accustomed to trust in the people around him. He gave us responsibilities, he put us in charge of missions, and one also always felt this trust as a healthy exigency. When he got upset, he got upset because we had done something wrong; nevertheless, a half hour later he was with us again making jokes as a way of showing us that everything was in the past. He is a man with a strong character, tenacious, but very generous.

In this house we had been advised about his many sides. First, as a Jesuit, the love he has for the Society, our order, which is our family. He taught us to love one another, reminding us that Jesuits, according to Saint Ignatius, are friends in the Lord. He taught us to be true friends, not mere co-workers. We have to be together especially in the difficult moments. He always said the religious order is like a family that goes well if the children, who are the youngest, are well cared for and protected and if the elderly are well looked after and respected.

As bishop, Pope Francis, when he had a sick priest, would be the first one to take care of him during the night. This attracted a lot of attention in Buenos Aires, among the priests, for the bishop to spend the night with a sick person, and he did it as if it were the most normal thing in the world because he had lived it here as a Jesuit every day.

Here he concerned himself with the care for the elderly, the sick, and he taught us to care for our brother Jesuits.

We have known a generation of brothers, meaning religious who are not priests and are dedicated to the work of the house, including the infirmary brother, the doorkeeper brother, the mechanic brother, and they were people of a notable spirituality and dedication. He taught us to care for them, to respect them, to learn from them.

Later we learned the pastoral dimension from him. He was pastor of a parish in Patriarca San José, which is a parish around here. He taught us to work, not to waste time, to take advantage of the little time we had on the weekend to go out and look for children in order to give them catechism classes, to knock on doors, to go visit the families, and so we ended up having a large number of children and youth.

When he was the superior of this house and pastor, he went camping near Mar del Plata with more than two hundred young people. Everything was paid for with donations that the students asked for during the year. To take a child who has never seen the ocean and who has never had a vacation was a way of giving him dignity, it was to consider him and treat him as a person, and even today they are young people who are now married, who have children, whom you can see at the parish, and they say, "Thanks to you, I saw the ocean, I went to the beach, I had a vacation once in my life." We also celebrated Children's Day, which we celebrated here with more than four thousand children, to whom we gave lunch, chocolate, and a little gift. He taught us that human dimension of the apostolate, of the mission, which permits us to comprehend that I cannot transmit the faith to a child if that child is hungry. One of his great works emerged in the same way, the kitchen for infants and the Casa del Niño, which cared for more than four hundred children each day, where there was not only food, but also medical attention and tutoring. We worked so that they would be educated, so that they would study to improve their situation. Another great project for which he provided the impetus was the night school for adults who had not finished high school. Thanks to this school, many young people and adults from the neighborhood completed their secondary education and could obtain a better job.

He also formed a technical school for young people to learn office skills ... these are projects from that time that show the extent of their apostolic value. He taught us not to be satisfied with doing a little but, rather, to ask ourselves: What more can we do so that people grow closer to God? With him we learned this apostolic zeal proper to the spiritual children of Saint Ignatius to try ourselves to reach and help another brother to help God.

*Shortly after being elected pope, some tried to link him to the military government's repression that followed the coup d'état in 1976 ...*

Everyone can have his own opinion, but beyond that, let us go to the testimonies of the people from that time. Let us see what the people say who were helped by Father Jorge, who was then a priest—not a bishop—to leave the country to save their lives.

We have the testimony, for example, of Alicia Oliveira,[1] who was helped by him in difficult moments when she was being persecuted. She tells how in our novitiate in San Miguel, young people were sheltered whom he later helped leave the country. But that is not going to be heard from Father Jorge, because he does not want to boast. There is

[1] Alicia Oliveira is an important Argentinean Judge who was dismissed from the bench, was persecuted and finally expelled from the country by the military dictatorship.

also a very important testimony from three priests from la Rioja, whose bishop, Bishop Enrique Angelelli, died in a very suspicious accident in 1976, which we are almost certain today was caused by the dictatorship. The bishop, shortly before, had brought three of his seminarians to finish their studies here in Colegio Máximo, because it was a way to protect them, because he trusted completely in Pope Francis, then Father Jorge Bergoglio, who was provincial. They were ordained priests in March 1978.

Other people have also given testimony of how they were helped. In fact, that includes the same Jesuit priests who were detained, Father Yorio and Father Jalics, who were freed through the negotiations he had with General Rafael Videla and Admiral Massera.

*How did you receive the news that Cardinal Bergoglio had been elected pope?*

When the pope was elected, I was listening to the radio at that moment, I just had turned on the radio; I was in my room, and while I was waiting for the announcement, the broadcasters were commenting. I was not very interested, because I had not learned that there had already been white smoke.

A few minutes later, the announcement was made and from that I made out the words "Cardinale Bergoglio", and I did not believe it. I thought I had heard wrong. Of course I ran to the television, where there were already others who were watching, and there was a deep sense of joy and at the same time sadness, because I felt like we had now lost him.

While he was archbishop of Buenos Aires, we were able to go visit him, to call him on the phone, it felt as though he were close, as if we had him right here. At that moment,

I told myself, "We have lost him; now he belongs to the whole world; now he is going to be in Rome; now we will not have him with us and for us." I know he himself was surprised, because, before he left he told one of the priests closest to him not to worry, that they were not going to elect him because with his age, there was no possibility. Immediately after the sadness, we started to perceive the joy of the people, and there came a true spiritual consolation, as if there were an atmosphere of fresh air in the Church, as if the people expected that the new pope would be able to inspire more enthusiasm in our Christian life.

I believe Pope Francis is responding on the basis of what is obviously a great pastoral background, greeting the youth and all people with that genuine smile. It is the same smile he had on August 7 in the Sanctuary of San Cayetano in Buenos Aires, where thousands of pilgrims visited the image of the saint, making a long line of at least two miles. He walked the line every year greeting each person personally.

I believe that now he understands that his ministry as successor of Saint Peter is for the people.

*Do you want to share some story in particular ...*

An almost incredible story from the life of the one who is now Pope Francis has to do with the image of the Mary, Undoer of Knots, or "Destanudos", that he brought from Germany. In December 1985, he ceased being the superior of this house and moved to the community of the Colegio del Salvador, our Jesuit community in Buenos Aires, and there he started his doctorate studies in theology, which he ultimately never obtained. As part of these studies, he traveled to Germany for six months, he studied German and investigated the figure of Romano Guardini, which was the subject he had chosen.

There he visited the city of Augsburg, where there is a Jesuit church called Saint Peter's, with the image of this Virgin, an image of the Immaculate Virgin, that is distinguished by the fact that the Virgin is undoing a ribbon with knots, which symbolizes the way in which the Virgin helps us undo, resolve problems, the difficulties in life. He really liked this image, and as it is common in churches in Europe, he bought some postcards with the picture of the Virgin and brought them back as gifts, as a remembrance of his trip.

A well-known person, dedicated to art, decided to make a copy of the image and give it as a present to a small parish in a neighborhood in Buenos Aires, in the Barrio de Argonomía. It is more or less in the center of the city of Buenos Aires. It was a small parish, with the normal flow of faithful, but when the pastor hung the image at the back of the church, more worshippers started to come and visit this image. Up to the point that currently, on the eighth of each month, thousands of pilgrims come to see the image. That is to say, the image he brought as a gift for some friends turned into a very popular devotion to the Virgin, which, as always happens with the Virgin, has done a lot of good, because thanks to her, many people have come back to the Church, have gone back to confession, have gone back to Communion.

He himself, reflecting upon what happened, told me once: "I have never felt myself so much an instrument in the hands of God; of having been a simple instrument." Because he never dreamed that the image of the Virgin that he had brought was going to turn into a popular Marian devotion and that it was going to do so much good for the people in Buenos Aires, and not only in the city of Buenos Aires, but also in the outskirts and in many other places where today this image is venerated.

# Eduardo Suárez

(dean of the Social Sciences Department at the Universidad del Salvador, friend of Pope Francis)

*How did you meet Pope Francis?*

I met him around the year 1974. I was a young college graduate at that time. As a young graduate, to be summoned to talk with the Father Provincial of the Society of Jesus in Argentina, who had directed the university where I was studying, had a very profound significance. And what was the first thing I saw? An absolute austerity in his way of living, in his manner of expressing himself, and in his behavior. An austerity that after many years is seen not to have varied in the least, despite the formalities that go along with his life, first, as a bishop and, later, in the last stage as a cardinal.

*Could you tell us how the Universidad del Salvador originated?*

The Universidad del Salvador was founded by the Jesuit fathers in the year 1956, following the long tradition of the Society of Jesus as to in the principles that inspired its creation. Argentina has had two universities from the Society of Jesus: the Universidad Católica in Córdoba and the Universidad del Salvador in Buenos Aires. In the beginning, the university had seven departments, and one of them was the Institute of Political Science, which later became the Department of Social Sciences.

*What was the role of Pope Francis in the development of the Universidad del Salvador?*

The current Pope Francis was named provincial of the Society of Jesus in the year 1973. He had two periods as provincial of the Society of Jesus: from '73 to '76 and from '76 to '79. During that time, the Society of Jesus made a decision, originating from the General, Father Pedro Arrupe, that entailed separating itself from some of the universities under its management. In this way, the Universidad del Salvador went from being founded by the Jesuits to being managed by a group of laymen. This transition took place in 1975, when Father Bergoglio was provincial of Argentina. For the transfer, Father Bergoglio presented the mission and objectives that the university ought to continue in order to respect its Catholic and Jesuit identity. Father Bergoglio conveyed to us, to those of us who were there at the beginning of this transition, the guiding principles of this house of studies. This was conveyed through a charter of principles, which were like the Magna Carta of the university. Some twenty years later, he himself delivered to us a new document, which reaffirms the guiding principles with which we started that new stage in 1975.

*What were the principal ideas that Father Bergoglio proposed?*

In that Magna Carta, he presented three great guiding principles, which are: first, the fight against atheism, with a strong emphasis on the spiritual dimension among the students. The second is unity through difference: he always thought that legitimate differences in the sphere of thought ought to be respected, always conserving unity. Lastly, intellectual advancement through a return to the source. That means, even though it appears contradictory, we need to advance while always looking back. Said in another way, the only way to advance is to be able to recognize the richness and the value present in the intellectual history of Catholicism. I believe that this principle can be seen today in Pope Francis. That obvious perspective in him is part of his rich personal history, and it has prepared him in some way for this mission of global magnitude.

He, Father Bergoglio, had a very important intellectual formation. These documents of which I am speaking, with which the identity of the university was given, clearly show that he not only proposes a priestly vision that provides a general orientation that's purely spiritual, but he also proposes, with direct words, various significant intellectual values with which we are summoned to work in this academic institution.

For example, he offered a very clear reflection about modern society and how the value of the person must be redeemed in this society, as if he had sensed the process of depersonalization in our urban societies, which was not perceived so clearly then. He also proposed, intellectually, generational reconciliation. Here we are talking about an interesting concept, which refers to generations that should not to relate to each other from a standpoint of conflict and rejection, but rather should maintain the sequence posed by the natural order of life and, of course, by the plan of God.

One of the things I remember most about this subject and that was most clear when I entered this prestigious institution in Argentina was something he asked the youth: to respect the elderly. In the second document he sent us twenty years later, this exhortation is recalled in this way: "Generational reconciliation must always exist."

Another thing that is laid down in this text is the correction of selfishness. Father Bergoglio perceived an individualist society, very concentrated in egoism, very hedonistic.

Faced with this challenge, he proposed that students receive a formation that allows them to comprehend that a profession, a job, is the giving of oneself, is service, is the transmission of values. Work is to form new generations in values and not in consumption. The pope also cautioned against things that historically continue to happen and warned of a society that is increasingly complex and increasingly individualistic.

*What aspects did he highlight on a spiritual level?*

I believe that there has always been continuity in his spiritual thought. One can see this process in his homilies and speeches, in those that reaffirm the importance of the transformation of the person as the basis for the existence of a community inspired by values and a society devoted to the destitute.

Personally, I can say that he has been the most important spiritual guide I have had throughout my life, in its various moments and stages. I was a young man of twenty-five when I met him. Now I am a man of more than sixty, one on whom his messages have had a varied impact. His message was one not only of words, but also of silence, of looks, of gestures. The spiritual teachings he transmitted to me and to many people came in the manner I have described, in the gestures that accompanied them, in the example as applied in his own life, and I believe we have to pay a lot of attention to these forms of communication.

*What did you feel when they announced the election of Pope Francis?*

I thought he was not going to be pope. Really, it was an absolute surprise, because he is an Argentinean, from a marginal place in the world, let us say. On one hand, the

history of the Church shows that popes are essentially Euro-
peans. Moreover, the media presented very different can-
didates ... but, well, the hand of the Holy Spirit was seen.
I believe that it remains clear that God's ways are still unpre-
dictable. I believe that even though we have statistics and
we can evaluate the pros and cons of people, sometimes
surprises continue to be very much a part of the sphere of
the Spirit.

*Have the first gestures from the pope surprised you?*

We are still at the beginning of his pontificate, but the gestures of his pontificate demonstrate in greater magnitude
the person his disciples have always known. For example,
for the pope, the most humble of people are equally important as the most important authorities or the famous. For
him, the man who sold the newspaper is just as important
as the Secretary of the United Nations. Be careful not to
be confused: this is not a "strategy" or a posture of the
pope; this shows him as he is; this shows what we have
always seen in him: that all people have the call and the
capacity for the spiritual life.

His gestures at the inauguration were surprising to some.
Maybe if they had not elected him, he would have gone
away completely unappreciated and there would have been
merely gestures in a local community "at the ends of the
earth", as he himself said.

Today we can see these little gestures, like the gesture of
washing the feet of prisoners in Rome, something he did
here as cardinal. Here, in fact, it did not have such a "strong"
meaning or so much exposure before the world. Ultimately, he continues being Father Bergoglio. I mean, he is
the pope, but one does not stop seeing who he is. Those of
us who have known him do not see only the pope or the

papacy today but, rather, the history of a man of faith who has gone through changes and growth but whose principles have remained intact during so many years.

*What effect does it have that he is a pope from Argentina and America?*

Argentina is a country of our Latin America with some unique characteristics. Maybe because we are a country that has had a more European population, from the beginning, unlike other countries that perhaps had much stronger native communities. But Argentinean Catholicism is ingrained in the history of Latin America. We have an almost common language in Latin America and the same faith. With some differences, we could say that of all America: they are people who still maintain the faith and the Gospel message.

I believe that this entails, in some form, a message to Europe, which is becoming more secular in an accelerated way, which originally preached the Gospel to the world but now transmits a completely different message to the rest of the world. In America, it is clear that the faith of our people is still present in the culture ... and that always is a source of hope, of much hope.

# Francesca Ambrogetti

(Italian journalist and co-author of the pope's biographical book *El Jesuita*)

*Tell us about the conversation with Cardinal Bergoglio about his life.*

It started with his vocation, marked by two distinct moments, because when he was close to death he was already a seminarian and had already started his priestly formation. He told us something very beautiful: he experienced great suffering, he really plunged to the depths of suffering, and everyone would say to him, "Don't worry, it will pass." These were phrases, he said, that "did not help me one bit, but what did help me was a nun who came to visit me and told me: you are imitating Jesus, the suffering of Jesus." That did help to ease his pain.

His vocation was revealed to him as something very strong, very important; he felt that God went in search of him; it was an intense moment. He says that he was going to go on an outing with his friends; before going he went to church and went to confession with a very spiritual priest ... and at that moment he felt the vocation so strongly that he did not go with his friends because he perceived that his life had changed. In those conversations he conveyed a great deal of faith, a very steady faith that he conveys to everyone.

He experienced the vocation when he was seventeen, which is very early. Now, in the pope's family, his grandmother was very happy, and his father as well, his mother not so much. His mother was not very happy and asked him to wait a little. In fact, he did wait a little between hearing the call and entering the seminary, but later he was very firm and did not turn aside for anything.

*What was the relationship like between the pope and his grandmother?*

His grandmother was a very important figure in his life. There is a chapter where there is an exchange of questions and quick answers: one of those questions was: A place? "Buenos Aires." A person? "My grandmother Rosa." His grandmother influenced him a great deal, and he has great admiration, great concern for the elderly; he always says that society must not discard them; it must care for them, attend to them. He has a real concern for them.

*What was it like when the pope was a schoolteacher?*

Not much is known. For me, he is a great educator. One of the most beautiful chapters of the book [*El Jesuita*] is the one devoted to education. It can be seen there that he has a deep interest in this subject. In the book, there is the testimony of one student, but we spoke with others; they liked him enormously. The students remarked that he was a very close companion, but strict. There is an episode in the book that is very interesting because there was a student who was very good but who had not finished his homework, and he had an exam and did an excellent job ... but he was given a nine and not a ten. This student told us: "I am never going to forget that lesson; I will be thankful for it the rest of my life." He was very loved by his students, and they themselves comment that the pope knew how to set limits and knew how to be a good educator.

*Some accuse the pope of being linked with the dictatorship. What can you tell us about it?*

That is written in the book; he tells about it there. He had never spoken about the issue, and he spoke about it in the book to which I refer. My testimony is that I would never have written this if I had had the slightest doubt, and because of these episodes, because of these things that have been said about him, a very large number of people have come forward who have said quite the opposite: these are people he helped. I deeply believe in that, and the rest is contained in the book.

*What is the origin of the book* El Jesuita*?*

It started on April 10, 2001. At that time I was the president of the Association for Foreign Correspondents, and Argentina was preparing for a crisis—it was in pre-crisis—that erupted in December 2001. I invited celebrities and relevant figures from different sectors to speak about the crisis, about the situation; and I saw that it would be important to know the opinion of the Church, which was already opening soup kitchens because there had already been a lot of poverty in Argentina. Jorge Mario Bergoglio had just been named cardinal and was the archbishop of Buenos Aires, the highest authority of the Church in Argentina. It seemed important to have him come speak with us, and the first impression I had was made by the fact that he personally answered the phone, without secretaries, without my having to pass through anyone; which is exactly what he is now doing in Rome. They say that he now calls and says "It's the pope." In those times, he would say "It's Father Bergoglio." He agreed to come to the meeting, and not only that. When I asked him if he was going to come in his car, he responded, "I do not have a car, I don't have a driver." So I told him, "Well, we will come get you." He then told me: "Do not come get me, I will take the bus, give me the address." He came, got out of the bus, and we saw him walking alone, dressed as a simple priest. That made such an impression that my foreign colleagues asked me, "But surely that is not the cardinal? Could it be his assistant?" Because he did not seem to be a cardinal; he came very simply; that is always his image ... he spoke in April 2001.

The meeting started, and he surprised us, because what he said about the Argentinean crisis and the world and the mission of the Church was so deep, so meaningful, so lucid. Before long, he had given us a valuable overview and had such an impact on the journalists that I said to myself, "Well, we have to go deeper. This person has a lot to say." The idea of these discussions arose there, but they then took five years to materialize because it was difficult; we proposed it, but he did not want to. He was always a very low-key person. Finally, the conversations materialized around 2007, and then the project continued, and the book came about.

*What was it like talking with the cardinal during those two years for the book?*

It was truly so enriching, I did not want to finish it. I always say that it was a difficult book to start and difficult to finish. We were not able to finish it because there were more subjects, and we did not want to finish because he was enriching us with his presence.

The conversations were very cordial, very sincere, and long, because each one lasted more than two hours, without interruptions. They always started with a short soccer anecdote. With Sergio Rubin, the co-author, we always spoke about soccer, joking around about it; and they always ended the same way, with him saying, "I hope it has been useful for you and that you have not wasted your time"; and our response was, "Time is not lost, it is gained with true spiritual enrichment." No one commissioned us to write the book. We did not know if they were going to publish it in the first version in 2010. We wrote it because we felt he was someone whose thought deserved to be known; the thought and the person.

*Why did you choose to include a homily-reflection from the pope on the Martin Fierro poem at the end of the book* El Jesuita?

Martin Fierro[1] is a gaucho poem, about an Argentinean cowboy; it is a very emblematic poem for Argentineans, the very essence of what this country is, at least in its origins. He is a person with Italian origins, with a great European culture. His family educated him in European culture; he feels very Argentinean and has chosen that as an emblem of what it is to be from this country. He makes interesting reflections about this subject, and we wanted to include it in the book. They are universal reflections that seem to me to be able to reach everyone. There are chapters from the book that speak only about Argentina, but there are certainly chapters that also can be a motivation and an example for other countries.

---

[1] *El Gaucho Martín Fierro* is a narrative book in verse written by the Argentinean author José Hernández in 1872. The work contains the wisdom of an imaginary cowboy who reflects about life, and many Argentinean critics consider it a metaphor of Argentinean history. It is considered by Argentineans to be an emblematic book of their country.

*What was most striking to you about the pope's life?*

There were many things; one of them was that moment of life and death, and what a great impact it had on him. Later, there was his teaching experience, about which he speaks very little. He was a teacher very much loved by his students, and when he speaks of his experience, he says a very beautiful phrase that has to do with what he is doing now; he says, "My students taught me to be more of a brother than a father." That brotherly attitude is what he is showing now. Then I would say it was that moment of faith, the moment he discovered his vocation; he talks about it very powerfully. This episode had a great impact on us. He described to us a time when he told a person who wanted to go to confession that he did not have time to hear his confession because he was leaving for a retreat, and he asked him to wait for another priest to come out to hear his confession. He left the cathedral, and then it hit him, and he said, "No, this is not my mission; I am a pastor; I have to ..." And he went back and heard the confession of that person ... You could tell how deeply he regretted not having wanted to hear the confession in the first place. Those are some of the many things that really drew our attention.

*Have the pope's gestures surprised you?*

For the people here who have known him well, there is no surprise. I would like to stress that if there is something to highlight, from those who know him, it is the complete coherence of his life. For those who know him— and I am talking about people who have truly known him for many years—there is no surprise. What he is doing is what he has always done, it is who he is; what he does is who he is. He has not changed; he is the same person.

*What other things do you believe are going to be surprising about the pope?*

Everybody says that he is a pope who will continue to surprise. It is not necessary for others to try to interpret him; he is the one who will speak. He speaks in the book, as he said later after being chosen to become a cardinal, about a Church that walks: that phrase is very beautiful; a Church that does not walk is a Church that is condemned to crumble like a sand castle. In the book, he also affirms that "a person who remains enclosed in his room suffocates." So, he speaks of a Church that cannot remain enclosed but that goes out; and when the Church goes out, she may discover surprises that will certainly be there, but he will be there marking this path, which is indispensable. The Church must walk; he has said it very clearly.

*Did you imagine that Cardinal Bergoglio was going to be elected pope?*

It was thrilling for me; everybody asked me if I imagined he was going to be pope, and Sergio Rubín and I and the authors say that, no, no, we never imagined it. When we worked on the book project, it was unimaginable, but whoever knew him perhaps might have thought that "he would be a good pope."

*Does Pope Francis like tango?*

We spoke about music, and he said that he really liked classical music. The title of that chapter is: "I Also Like Tango."

He also likes tango, which he danced as a young man, but he prefers milonga.[2] I think that has to do precisely with his Argentinean identity. It has to do with having roots in another place but holding on to roots from a new place; that explains his emotional connection to Martin Fierro, tango, or the neighborhood soccer team.

*How do you see him with respect to his affection for sports, for soccer, and for the San Lorenzo soccer club?*

In general, that is very typical of an Argentinean. What Argentinean does not have a soccer team? It was his neighborhood's team, it was where his father brought him as a child to play basketball, and it also has to do with porteño[3] identity, the Buenos Aires identity, and truly he has a lot of affection for it, it is very human. All of this shows a human figure who is very intelligent, very spiritual, but at the same time very human, very much with his feet planted on the ground.

*How do you think being Argentinean with Italian parents will influence the pope?*

There is a phrase from Borges[4] that is true—because many things attributed to Borges are not from him. He said "I do not feel completely Argentinean because I do not have one

[2] Milonga is an Argentinean musical genre, less well known internationally than the tango but very popular in and around Buenos Aires. Its origin can be traced back to the African slaves, but it acquired a more urban and sentimental character in the beginning of the twentieth century.

[3] Porteño means "from the port". It is a term used to refer to the people and the cultural forms of Buenos Aires, especially in the neighborhoods close to the port.

[4] Argentinean author Jorge Luis Borges (1899–1986), noted for his short stories, poetry, and essays.

drop of Italian blood in my veins." Because the Italian really influences the Argentinean. If we turn the phrase around, Bergoglio could say, "I feel completely Argentinean because I have 100 percent Italian blood in my veins." So that is exactly what it has to do with; the homeland, which comes from the father, who is clinging to this new homeland, and he says that his father, although born in Italy, put aside his nostalgia or concealed it in order to cling to his new nationality ... This is very typical of an immigrant, the son from a family of immigrants who takes to his new homeland, where he grows and develops with much force and with much love.

*How was Cardinal Bergoglio with the poor, with the "forgotten"?*

That was continuously seen; he showed it in gestures, in attitudes, in words; he speaks a lot with his gestures, but he has a great vocation to the neediest, a great sensitivity. Someone asked me what would be the quality that I would most highlight; it is difficult to decide on only one, but one is his sensitivity, his attentiveness to the other person, his listening, being sensitive to what the other person needs. He worked a lot in prisons, something that is not very well known. He went to hospitals a lot; he went to the retirement homes; he went to the priests' retirement home to visit them; they were alone, and he went to visit them. He stands out for always having approached the neediest.

*And his spiritual side?*

The gesture of asking the people to pray for him right after he was elected did not surprise anyone in Argentina who knew him, because in all his meetings, in his encounters,

he would say that to practically everyone, asking them—whoever it was—to pray for him. If it was a group, he would tell them, "pray for me." If it was a person, he would ask him informally: "Pray for me." And also in his letters—many people who have received his letters have told me this—he always tells them: "Pray for me."
It is a great gesture of true humility. The first time he said that to me, I felt very surprised because, if anything, he should pray for the other person, but that is how he first demonstrates his confidence in prayer, the value he gives to prayer from the other person, and the importance that the spiritual life has for him.

*Do you have some favorite story about Pope Francis?*

I have one that I tell because it is one of the most important. It demonstrates exactly who he is. This anecdote was told to me firsthand by a journalist, a colleague from the newspaper *La Nación* whose name is Jorge Ruillón. I just saw him yesterday, and he told me, "Tell them whatever you want" because I think that, among so many, it is marvelous and very emblematic. This journalist who was about to have some medical tests done and was a little bit worried ran into him. So he tells him, "Father Bergoglio—he liked to be called Father Bergoglio—can I ask you a favor: pray for me because I am going to have some medical tests done, and I am a little worried, so please pray for me", and he tells him that he will. They do the medical tests, and in the end everything turns out fine, and he completely forgets about the issue. Two or three months later, he happens to meet Cardinal Bergoglio, and the cardinal says to him, "Tell me, can I stop praying for you now?" The journalist is shocked. The protagonist had forgotten about it, but the cardinal had remembered and had continued praying. This anecdote shows the great attention he has for the other person and, at the same time, his memory—he really remembers things well. I choose this anecdote because I think it is one of the most significant, but there are many more.

*How do you see the subject of the family in the pope's thinking?*

It is very central, both in regard to his family background—his own family was marked a lot by the figure of his grandmother—and in terms of what the family is in general. When he speaks about education, he speaks a lot about the family. When he speaks about free time or when he speaks about the dignity of work, he always speaks in reference to family life.

This sends a strong message, so much so that a mother told me that, "having read his book, it really struck me that parents should play a lot with their children, that they should speak with their children, that they should be with their children, that they should share with their children. Today parents have very little time for sharing, and that is at times the source of many family problems."

*And the defense of life?*

Yes. It has not been a subject that was discussed a lot, but of course he promotes an unyielding defense, an absolute defense of life. It was a theme that is touched on in the book, but not very deeply, precisely because for him it is something undisputed, beyond all discussion.

In one chapter he speaks specifically about that and says: "We must preserve life from conception until death." Here we go back to the same thing: it is useless to preserve life and then later let those children die from starvation or allow the elderly to be abandoned. Few say it. Many speak of the fight against abortion and all of that, but the defense of the child after conception must also be promoted, when he is small and also when he is growing up. Meaning that he supports the defense of life always, certainly he is completely against abortion, but he is in defense of life always.

*How does Pope Francis see the future?*

This is the big question, which I do not consider myself to have sufficient authority to answer, so I have to recall his own words: A Church that is not going to sit still, a Church that is not static. We can be sure that this is going to be the Church of Pope Francis, remembering that he said that "the person who stays enclosed in his room suffocates."

He speaks a lot about a Church that is not self-referential, of a Church that goes out to encounter the people, that searches, that is missionary and pilgrim. I think that this is going to be his path. On this path, the pope is going to listen to the signs from the world and from the Church, and he is going to act accordingly and faithfully.

# Etelvina Sánchez

(sixty-two years old, a beggar who is frequently around the cathedral in Buenos Aires)

*How did you meet Pope Francis?*

I met him when he came walking through here on the sidewalk. He always greeted me "Etelvina", and I greeted him. I met him when my daughter was four years old . . . now she, and her name is Cecilia, she turned twenty-one on March 14. I wear this rosary on top [around her neck] because Father [Bergoglio] always told me: "Pray for me." So, at night I always take my rosary and pray a bit, even though I don't know it very well . . . but he always encouraged me to "pray, pray."

*When he would tell you: "Pray for me . . ."*

"Yes, Father, I will pray for you"—I would tell him. I called him Father; I never said Bishop or Cardinal, I saw that he was like that, close, a father . . . Well, he always passed by on the sidewalk at ten or eleven in the morning. I was here, seated, "Good-bye, Father", I would say to him, and he would come down, and I would greet him. And he would stop, and we would talk a bit, and each time when it was time for him to go, he would always say to me: "Pray for me, alleluia." Sometimes he would laugh, "I know I always say the same thing"; because he always told me: "Pray for me." And now, he has to pray for us, right? I know he now prays for us.

*What did you feel when they elected him pope?*

I did not know whether to cry or to laugh. In the beginning, I was happy, and at the end I was very sad, because now that he is pope I am not going to be able to see him again. Because he cared for me, he cared for us, he knew all of us. I have several daughters: one is in the capital, she got into tourism; another is studying; and another is here with me, the one who has a little boy, and since the baby does not have a father, the child is with me, he lives with me. The twenty-one-year-old is looking for work and has not been able to find any, and she has been looking for a while.

I have hope that the pope is going to come one day, and I am going to greet him, with arms wide open. Because being a priest or a bishop, it always struck me, because he was really loved. I always liked to greet him because he always gave a smile. He never greeted seriously or in a bad mood, he always passed by here with a smile, and I like people who smile. I do not like angry people, that is just how I am. I get rather angry when I get upset. When I am fine, well, I am fine. We miss him here. I am going to turn sixty-three years old, and the bishop would have given me a gift ... I hope he sends me a gift from Rome ... I know he will remember me because I appreciate him a lot, I love him a lot.

# Rabbi Abraham Skorka

(friend of Pope Francis and co-author of the book *On Heaven and Earth*)

*How did your friendship with Pope Francis begin?*

The Jewish community in Argentina is the first community in terms of numbers in the region and in the Jewish culture that was developed here. The Latin American Rabbinic Seminary, of which I have been director for many years, has its main campus in Buenos Aires, where we form our teachers of Hebrew and Jewish tradition. We export rabbis to all of Latin America, from Mexico to Peru. Many German Jews arrived here after the Second World War and created institutions like this one where we are seated at this moment [the Berkel Tikva Community Synagogue in Buenos Aires].

The circumstances under which I met Cardinal Bergoglio had to do with some public events. The national holidays on which we remember the independence of Argentina are two: May 25 and July 9; the first one is the "Cry for Freedom", and the second is when the Argentinean independence was formally proclaimed, establishing the nation. On these occasions, there is a traditional religious service held in the [Catholic] cathedral, where the president of the nation also invites other creeds. Since Argentina has a very strong Roman Catholic and apostolic tradition, the *Te Deum* is prayed in the Metropolitan Cathedral, and representatives from different creeds accompany the act, greeting, according to protocol, the different authorities. In the nineties, the president made a change and used to invite me to participate in these acts. It was in the second half of the nineties, as I recall, when Jorge Mario Bergoglio first became the coadjutor archbishop and then the archbishop of Buenos Aires, that we started to get to know each other. He had referenced me for various articles I wrote in the newspaper, and I had a little television program in the evening where I spoke about Judaism for a few minutes to close the program on a television channel he also watched. So, we saw each other, and we greeted each other, until one time he asked something that is very common here in Argentina and especially in Buenos Aires, "What's your team?" Meaning, of what soccer team are you a fan? He told me he was for San Lorenzo, a team founded by a priest, and it was logical that he would be a fan even today; and I told him that I was for River. When River was not doing well and San Lorenzo was doing well, he started to make some jokes with me, and I saw he was a different man, a man who tried to draw close to his neighbor, one with whom he could begin to walk along a path of deep rapprochement, real and serious interreligious dialogue.

*What was the interreligious dialogue like with the then archbishop of Buenos Aires?*

The path consisted of various actions with which we began to see that there was a predisposition to work, taking increasingly stronger steps to craft a message to the entire Argentinean society: that Jews and Catholics must walk together, because we have a common beginning.

The relationship between Christianity and Judaism is much deeper than could exist between Christianity and Islam or between Christianity and any other religion that we know in the world. Why? Because originally, at a moment in history, within a people, within the Jewish people, a dialogue started to form between two families. One is this circle that was formed around Jesus, a primordial circle from which Christianity was formed, and the other is Rabbinic Judaism.

Of course Islam also places its roots inside the Hebrew Bible, from the Hebrew tradition, and also later passes through Christianity, but from the point of view of Jewish history, it is a secondary step. The first is that which unites Jews and Christians, in this case the Roman Catholic and Apostolic Church, which is the most important in the country.

With Archbishop Bergoglio, we felt committed, first, because we were able to walk together and we had to walk together, each one with his identity, but trying to form a spiritual and peaceful message for Argentina, for the City of Buenos Aires and, at the time, for the world.

In 2001, John Paul II made him cardinal, and then he wanted to organize—and he, in fact, did organize it—acts for peace in those dark and shadowy days before the war with Iraq, shadowy because all war is shadowy, because war is anti-human. And then a prayer for peace was made. He invited me, and later, at times when we wanted to do something relevant, we called each other. When I wanted—for example, here in this same temple in 2004 and again in 2007 before the High Holy Days, [Jewish] New Year and Kippur—to show a presence and obtain a Catholic message for the Jews, before an important spiritual moment like the prayer asking for God's forgiveness, I invited him so that as archbishop of Buenos Aires he would give us a message, and it was something very important.

It was the first time that an archbishop gave a message in a temple to the Jewish community, and a message that was not merely "I wish you a Happy New Year" but, rather, a deep message, a message in which he spoke from his heart, from our common roots as he perceives them, to his older brothers.

For Pope Francis, in fact, the concept of "older brother" is an important concept, but, besides being concrete, it is fraternal. That is why, when two journalists finished writing his biography,[1] he himself suggested, without thinking twice, that the introduction be done by me. This shows the concept of brotherhood between Jews and Catholics.

*How did the idea of the book* On Heaven and Earth *arise?*

We got to know each other. Ours is not a superficial friendship; it is not only a "I will invite you to coffee, and we will chat about life." Whenever we got together, we always asked ourselves, "What are we doing so that there is a little bit more spirituality in the world?" Walking together, we would always ask each other, "What is our next plan?", "What is our next mission?"

Mission, plans ... Projects!—that would perhaps be the most accurate word, "What is our next project?" And, well ... that is how the book arose. I wanted to write a book about theological issues with a chapter written by him, but he wanted something different, a book about subjects that affect everyone, the people, the man in the street.

We did it together with a journalist, and Bergoglio always told him: "ask without fear, ask, ask more incisive questions without any type of restriction. Afterward, we will polish it, we will polish the text, but you ask." When we were alone, we spoke with a very great degree of spiritual closeness. There was a respect and spiritual interchange that was always very intense.

[1] *El Jesuita*, written by journalists Sergio Rubin and Francesca Ambrogetti in 2010 and republished after Cardinal Bergoglio's election as pope.

To prepare the book, we met once a month for a whole year. We placed a table right here on Tuesday or Wednesday at nine in the morning. At that time the cardinal would arrive. I had offered to go to his office in the center, but he would tell me, "You do not need to cross the city to go to my study. I am going to go to your temple."

He is a little bit older than I, and nevertheless he would tell me, "I am coming, I will take the subway." And he came down here to about four blocks away, and he walked the rest ... yes, the archbishop of Buenos Aires. We had some very good croissants that they prepare here, and so in this intimate and familiar area we worked out many chapters of the book.

Once the book was finalized, what was the next project? A television program. For two straight years. How did we do this program? We met, and we decided to talk, for example, about happiness or disagreements between brothers and sisters or a family. We made the program with an Evangelical named Marcelo Figueroa, who was the moderator and who introduced the topic, and that is what produced the dialogue between us.

It was a program that was rerun several times on the archdiocese's channel and that many people watched. It penetrated deeply, and people on the street would say to us "Congratulations on the program." It was, however, something "silent", without great advertisement in the media. With the pope, we looked each other in the eye and were able to have a dialogue about concepts, and we were able to think about what the other said and see how to complement it or how to show an alternative vision: showing what we agreed about, in what aspects we had different perspectives, and always with total and absolute respect.

On the topic of abortion, for example, the Jewish norms are more flexible than the Catholic ones. Nevertheless, what unites us, of course, is the holiness of life, the respect that the life of each individual deserves, the respect that the unborn being deserves. The program wanted to demonstrate to society what it meant to have a dialogue, because we have lost the capacity for dialogue in our country. It is now common to have, as the archbishop of Buenos Aires used to say at the time, a situation of tension instead of dialogue. People tense up and immediately stop talking. A tense person loses the capacity to make his case, to explain an idea with tranquility.

*What was it like for you when you learned that your friend, the archbishop of Buenos Aires, had been elected pope?*

Even though the media said that he was not *papabile*, I did think that he could become pope. The news did not surprise me, because he has a really towering spiritual level. I remember that in the previous election, he found widespread acceptance and received a lot of support to become pope because of this spiritual and intellectual level, and he was seriously considered by many cardinals, especially from America. In the meeting in Aparecida,[2] with the bishops and the pope in Brazil, he had some very important interventions. That is why [his election] did not surprise me.

Now, when I saw him come out on the balcony on television, I was able to see him face to face, remembering that he worked a lot with those gestures, looking us in the eye and speaking to us not only with words but also with silence. It was very touching, seeing that face and suddenly the image

---

[2] The Fifth General Conference of the Bishops of Latin America and the Caribbean took place from May 13–31, 2007, in the Marian Sanctuary in Aparecida, Brazil. It was inaugurated by Pope Benedict XVI. Cardinal Bergoglio was responsible for the drafting commission and had a prominent role during the conference.

dressed in white ... I realized that my friend who could call me on the telephone at any time, just as I could call him, was now going to stay in Rome. Already, as pope, he has called me on the telephone, and he told me a joke at the beginning of the call: "Look, Skorka, they are not letting me leave Rome. I arrived here, they grabbed me, and they will not let me go back." We left many things in the pipeline here, but that is up to God; we also spoke about that during the phone call.

*Were you at the installation in Rome?*

No, no, I was not, even though people from the Rabbinic Seminary wanted to send me to Rome and even accompany me ... but Pope Francis had asked Argentineans, instead of traveling, to give money to the poor. When we spoke, I told him, "Look, I did not go to the installation, because I did what you asked, I helped the poor." I did not go despite the fact that they offered to accompany me and coordinate all the details of the trip.

I was moved that he called me the day of the Mass that initiated his pontificate, a few hours before. He himself told me, "God will give us the opportunity to continue our tradition; the moment we get together, I am sure we are going to sit down, we are going to look at each other, and we are going to say: What should we do? What is our next project?"

I know he has a lot of work to do, but perhaps I can still suggest some project to him. When we see each other, I know it will not be a matter of only embracing and taking a picture. With him, we have done many committed things, and I greatly appreciate how much he did for Judaism in general.

That is my story with Bergoglio.

# Father José María "Pepe" di Paola

(fifty years old, priest of the "slums", friend of Pope Francis)

*What was your experience like working closely with Cardinal Bergoglio in the slums?*

The experience with Cardinal Bergoglio was really very good. First, he was the one who assigned me to work in the slums. I think I had already been a priest for many years and had worked a lot with young people. The poorest neighborhoods were his great concern, and he was the one who assigned me to Villa 21,[1] for work that was carried out in a shanty town that is called Ciudad Oculta, which is also a slum.

From that time on, I carried out the work, always in the company of the cardinal and of a group of priests who tried to intervene so that children did not fall into drugs or some kind of violence. He was always with us in our reflection and in the work we did.

*How did Cardinal Bergoglio relate with the people in the slums?*

It was characteristic of the cardinal to let us work with freedom, and he himself also moved around freely. He would come at any moment, above all in the beginning, when he

---

[1] Villa 21 is part of Barracas, a marginalized urban neighborhood in Buenos Aires. It is the *villa miseria*—a term used in Argentina to describe extreme urban poverty—with the highest population and worst reputation for violence in the capital of Argentina.

did not have so many obligations, having only recently become archbishop of Buenos Aires. He might come to a Mass where we invited him to celebrate the sacraments of Christian initiation, or he might also come to drink maté with a group and chat.

I remember he came sometimes without telling us in advance simply to work in the streets of the slum, to meet people. If there is something that could be singled out about him, and I never get tired of repeating it, it is that for him the center of Buenos Aires is not the Plaza de Mayo, where the power resides, but, rather, the outskirts of the city.

As bishop of Buenos Aires, he always sought out these places; a bit forgotten by those in power, they are really the center. That not only helped the people of these neighborhoods improve their condition, but the rest of the city of Buenos Aires also saw these neighborhoods in a different way. I think this was very important in what we call the integration of the city.

*What was your personal experience of friendship like with the pope?*

The experience for me was really that of a very important spiritual father. He is someone who was with us and was with me at every moment: moments of hope at the beginning of a project, like the one I am starting here now [in the Villa de la Carcova] from zero, there we also started without anything. To accomplish these projects, to be with us in doing them ... the congeniality of working in a community with people from the neighborhood and with other priests from other slums. Happy moments—of the inauguration of a training center of offices for Hogar de Cristo and of a rehabilitation center for addicted children. There are also tense and difficult moments, like when we were threatened, in which he was always at our side, with us, making the best of it. So, that is how we established a very close relationship.

*How did the pope help you when you received death threats?*

The priests in the slums wrote a document in which we revealed the great difficulties suffered by the children and youth in our neighborhoods. We have children and youth that grew up very well, and suddenly we would find them thrown out on the street; they started to run away from home, from their life's work, school, clubs, their very parish, and we were saying, "What is happening here?"

It was the "paco" invasion, a very destructive drug that is derived from cocaine and was cheap, which got into their humble world, into their marginal world, and it caused these children to become a great worry for us and for their parents. So, we wrote a document to share with society; in fact, we promoted it through the media, in which we said, "Drugs in the slums are decriminalized, in fact, and we are increasingly worse off."

We passed on what we lived and saw. People thanked us, saying, "Father, thank you for saying this publicly because it is what we as parents are suffering." Or the addicts themselves would say to you, "Pepe, how good of you to speak about this because we know how it happens ..." Society started to speak about this topic, but even though many were happy, there was a small group who saw that their interests were at stake. So, then came the threats. They threatened me with death repeatedly, maybe for being the coordinator of the group of priests in the slums.

The first time was a day when I was riding my bike. A person stopped me and said that I did not know him, that I was going to be killed—here he said "bumped off." "You're going to be bumped off." I was a little confused because I thought the person was going to ask me something like any other person in the neighborhood, when was this, that, or some other course, and I told myself, "Tomorrow I will speak with the cardinal."

So, I went the next day, and I told him, "Look, Cardinal—we say Boss, joking with him—they have threatened to kill me, and I think it could be serious." In fact, afterward I started to receive text messages, letters, meaning it was a serious thing. So, he put his hands on his head, and I remember that he sat down, and I remember the phrase that came out: "I am really going to ask God that if something has to happen, it happens to me and not to you." So, that left me very ... like saying, "This man is asking God that if somebody has to die, it will be him and not me." He said it from his heart because he was saying it only to me, because there was nobody else around to look good in front of. The next day, in the Plaza de Mayo, the Mass of the Catholic schools was celebrated, and he denounced what had happened. He knew that the way to protect me had to do with letting society know. Many times the mafia is successful precisely because of fear or because they move around like that, in the shadows. That made the media support me a lot in the sense that people knew I had been threatened.

The people backed me. Closing down the street, people spontaneously put together a very big march and invited me to it. I had not organized it, inside the slums. The people in the slums reacted as they always do, in a very positive way.

On Sunday, a Mass was celebrated, also with many people. The presence of the cardinal was very committed. There were difficult times, but I never felt alone, because friends, the people of the slums, people also from other places, people from society in general, and above all my bishop were beside me.

*Do you have some special memory of the pope in the slums?*

The cardinal has attitudes that today surprise the world. We were also surprised at the time, but for him they are common. I mean that his friendly treatment of others, which is simple, uncomplicated, and very austere, makes people feel very close to him.

I remember something a boy said to me who was working on a building site. The majority of the population of the slums are builders, they go and work on construction sites. One day, a bus full of people came to the slums. There is a bus that goes close to the cathedral, and then you see the cardinal come in that bus, and he was going to get off there.

Suddenly, this boy says, "There goes our bishop." And the other boys got into the bus with him, and they could not believe it. They say, "Let's go, let's go to ask for a blessing." They approached and asked for a blessing; one of them introduced himself, saying, "I am from Villa 21, I am from the group of men from the parish were Father Pepe is." The cardinal gave him and the others the blessing. They got off and could not believe it. The next Sunday they came to Mass. That testimony of closeness really made an impact on them, seeing the cardinal travel "the same way we travel."

I remember, also, one time, in a part of the slum that is called Zavaleta, we were putting together a stage, a rather fragile stage, because we were building it with empty beer boxes, with wood on top, and we had to put it together for a Mass and later for a festival. Bergoglio did not come, and we said, "What could have happened to him? Could he have forgotten? How strange, a person who writes everything down." Well, after an hour we did not know where he was, and we saw him come out in the middle of the slum, from a house. And we asked him, "What were you doing?" And he told us, "No, I arrived, and you were working, and the people asked me to bless their houses, so I went and blessed them." The cardinal always surprised us with those visits and with his very spontaneous way of saying, "You were working, I will continue doing my things and let you work."

The people did not know he was the bishop. We are talking about many years ago, and they thought he was just a priest who came to help. He went to bless the houses, and later the people were surprised when during the Mass he put on all of the bishop's attire. For the people from the Zavaleta neighborhood, that was very important, and they always talk about it.

That is why there are many people who are very touched about his being pope . I saw it in them the other day when we were at the vigil in the Plaza de Mayo for the pope's installation. The people from the slums carried pictures of themselves drinking maté with him, pictures in which he is confirming them ... that is to say, different types of pictures that speak of beautiful moments in their life with the one who is now the pope, moments they will never forget.

*So he was as close as they say ...*

Yes, it was always like that. He is a person who likes to share the simple moments of the lives of other people. He felt very comfortable. You could see him arrive in the slums, I remember him getting off bus 70, on [the corner of the intersection of] Iriarte and Luna, and walking all those blocks, and along the way he would meet people. For him, that was the most beautiful moment, so that I would say that the slums and sanctuaries, for him, were the places where he felt most comfortable.

*What did you feel when they elected him pope?*

First, surprise, because in the last election we thought he could become pope. In this one, it caught us by surprise, and we felt happy because we know he is a person who can contribute what the people are hoping for from the Church. In fact, we now are informed by the newspapers or by the testimonies of people from other countries—not only here in Argentina, but also people from other countries, from Europe, from our Latin American countries, from the United States itself—that there is joy and a strong spiritual momentum thanks to this choice by God in the figure of our Bishop Bergoglio. So, I think we have what is needed to provide what people are searching for in the Church. I believe that his testimony in the poor neighborhoods, where there are problems like drugs, helps priests, religious, and laypeople in different parts of the world, with these same problems or worse, discover now a pope who is close to them.

So, I believe that this is, for me, the great contribution of Cardinal Bergoglio, and another important thing is that for him, as for us, a poor person is not only a person who needs to be helped. Obviously, it is a person who needs to be helped, because that is the commandment of love, but also a person from whom we must learn. Let us remember that phrase of Jesus, which says, "I praise you, Father, because you have revealed these things to the small and not to the wise and prudent."

*According to the current pope, how should a priest from the slums be?*

The priests live in the slums. So the Church has a view from inside the slum. The State was absent for forty years or so, so what happened? The slum did not have a school, it did not have a police station, it did not have a court, there was no university, there was nothing; but, yes, there was a chapel.

So, the Church had a view from the people. I think that this was a great contribution we can always make. We have to understand that violence and marginalization occur when the State is not present. You then have a society that neglects a large part of itself, with many city blocks where there are no lights, where there is no asphalt, where a police patrol does not go, where the ambulance does not go, where people go unprotected.

We have a document where we speak about the cultural identity of the slums, all the values that the city of Buenos Aires itself and other neighborhoods have lost. You go to Buenos Aires, or any other neighborhood, and you are going to say, "The Parque Patricios used to be so beautiful! How beautiful Palermo used to be! Let's get together to eat, to chat on the streets and play soccer." Today that has been lost. Today, this is lived in the slums, because the slums conserve the community identity. That is why, in addition to evangelizing, we try to develop preventive and restorative work. This is similar to the method of Saint John Bosco: making it so that the chapels and the community centers that we have inside the slums might be places where children can grow in a healthy way. So, from childhood through adolescence, the child is raised in a Church that is with him.

We have achieved many things through sports, from camping programs to academic support to job training programs. In some slums we have constructed primary and secondary schools. We seek to protect the life of the child so that he can grow up healthy, but we do not forget about the child who unfortunately got into drugs, who went into that parallel world and dropped out of school, left his family, and stopped going to the chapel . . .

Today, we have three rehabilitation centers in Villas 21, in Bajo Flores, and in Retiro. They are three very big slums, which have around 120,000 inhabitants, and with these centers they have the possibility of rehabilitation that is not given in other places.

*What impact do you think it will make on the people in the slums to have Cardinal Bergoglio as pope?*

Well, it has already made an impact on them; there is already great joy; the people here have a feeling that this is the Slum Pope, that is what they call him; that is what it says on a poster in our chapel, brought by people from Villa 21. It is a fact that the poorest people are very happy about the election of Francis. This is what should make us all happy. Like he always said, when the simplest people are happy, everyone else should also be happy. They are happy because they have experienced him, not as someone distant, but rather as someone very close who is now leading the Church.

# Oscar Luchini

(layman, sixty-nine years old, in charge of San Lorenzo de Almagro Soccer Club's chapel)

*What is Pope Francis' relationship with San Lorenzo?*

Our origin dates back to a Salesian priest, our founder, Father Lorenzo Massa, so we have a Catholic beginning. Jorge Bergoglio's father was a basketball player; he played on the Avenida de la Plata, where we used to have our headquarters, and Bergoglio, from the time he was very little, has been a fan of San Lorenzo.

He was not a member until he was already grown, when he was older, but he always came with his father. He came to watch the basketball games, soccer, and he became a supporter of San Lorenzo. We have had a relationship with him since he was a bishop and, later, cardinal. So, then a more direct relationship started with our club, but he was not a member until around 2007 or 2008; the president at that time proposed that we make him a member. He always paid his dues up until a little while ago, when they made him an honorary member. From that time on, he never paid, but, with his humility, he always wanted to help out with the club.

*What was the Centennial Mass of the club like?*

In 2008 we celebrated the Centennial Mass in the chapel of San Antonio, off Mexico Street in the Almagro neighborhood where San Lorenzo was founded. He celebrated the Mass as bishop along with other priests. Of course he came by bus and did not let us come to get him or take him home after the Mass. He was always like that.

In 2010, we had then finished the chapel, and so we invited him again to celebrate the Feast of Mary Help of Christians, our patroness, which is May 24. May 24, 2012, he came to celebrate here, in this chapel. That day I ventured to call him up on the phone, and I said to him: "Bishop, allow me to come get you, because it is raining cats and dogs, and you will not be able to get here; it is going to be very difficult for you to reach the sports center; you are going to be soaked; you are going to get dirty", and well ... that time he allowed me to get him; if it had not been for those circumstances, he would not have agreed. I went to get him in that little car which is sitting over there, which is a tiny little car and which a local sports magazine described as the "first popemobile", as a joke, but also as a testimony to his humility.

*How was it that this chapel was constructed next to the San Lorenzo stadium?*

This chapel was donated by an American-Argentinean, Viggo Mortensen,[1] because he lived a long time in our country and is also a supporter of San Lorenzo. The chapel was finished in 2010, and since then every Mass for the club has

---

[1] Viggo Peter Mortensen is a Hollywood actor of Danish decent who was raised in Argentina. He became famous with his role as Aragorn in the *Lord of the Rings* trilogy and also as an agent in *Eastern Promises*, for which he received an Oscar nomination. Mortensen is a supporter of the San Lorenzo Soccer Club, and even though he was raised Lutheran, he donated money for the construction of the club's Catholic chapel.

been celebrated in this place. As is known, Pope Francis celebrated a Mass here for the club's anniversary.

*Can you tell us the story of the shirt that has the pope's image on it?*

The pope was elected on Wednesday, and San Lorenzo was playing the following Saturday against Colón, in the province of Santa Fe. Then somebody mentioned that we should put him on a shirt. We asked the authorities at the AFA [Argentinean Soccer Association], and they authorized us for one time to put Pope Francis' picture on the shirt, because FIFA does not allow club shirts to have images during a sporting event, nothing that alludes to politics or to religion. That time they made an exception, and for that game they allowed it. We won the game of course.

*Can this shirt be used again?*

No, no, it cannot be used again. I suppose that someone will make some copy of it, but the club cannot go back to using it officially. At that time, they made thirty shirts. One was donated to the chapel, another was donated to the club, and others were auctioned for charities requested by the pope.

*What does it mean for San Lorenzo that the pope is a fan and that he has greeted them at an audience in Rome?*

Well, for us it is always tremendously important. While San Lorenzo de Almagro is a great club of the Argentinean Republic, it is not that well known. From now on, with the pope, that has changed. People have come here from all over the world, even Arab countries, to film. That was just in the week when the pope was installed.

*How do you see the fans in relation to the pope?*

Thanks be to God, they are very peaceful, because it is one of the things that the pope asks of us. That is the reason for the chapel, to struggle with the sea from the inside, to bring the fans in. You know that every soccer club has real problems with drinking, and here we are working so that these things do not go any farther down the wrong path, so that these types of problems do not arise, and little by little we are going to achieve it. That is the motive for the chapel, to calm the fans, to bring them to God and the real meaning of sports, like the pope says, like he always told us.

# Liliana Negre

(pro-life and pro-family senator who continually consulted with Cardinal Bergoglio)

*What was your contact like with Cardinal Bergoglio?*

First of all, I am Catholic; that influences my entire life and my political actions. I entered the Senado de la Nación, on March 14, 2001, when out of seventy-two senators, only three of us were women. I was born into an absolutely, practicing Catholic family. I belong to the Peronista Party, and I have had a Cabrinian formation. The Sisters of the Sacred Heart, founded by Saint Frances Xavier Cabrini[1]—patroness of immigrants—formed me. She personally founded the school in my province and in my city. So, that is how I have a deeply Catholic formation. I was, moreover, in the Major School of the Sisters of the Immaculate Virgin, meaning that I have had the witness of my parents, a Catholic formation in school, and later I was concerned about deepening this formation.

I had the honor of being the first president of Acción Mundial de Parlamentarios por la Vida y la Famila [Parliamentarians and Governors for Life and Family], which gathers members from forty-three countries. Today I am the

---

[1] Saint Frances Xavier Cabrini (1850–1917), Italian religious founder of the Missionaries of the Sacred Heart and patroness of immigrants, traveled tirelessly through the United States helping immigrants both materially and spiritually. Her zeal for the spiritual health of immigrants even brought her to Costa Rica, Brazil, Chile, Panama, and Argentina, where her community prospered in a special way.

honorary president. I have also had the honor, in the last
two family congresses, to have been invited by the Vatican
as a speaker, as a world speaker in defense of life and the
family. It is obvious that as a Catholic, with my own authority and because of my position, I would have sought the
advice of the Church leadership, in this case, until recently,
Cardinal Jorge Mario Bergoglio.

*You became famous in the Hispanic world by being the senator
who made the surprise announcement that the new pope was
Argentinean.*

The truth is that there are no coincidences. I believe that it
was Providence that placed me in that moment, because
we have a television in our offices, and when we were preparing to go into session, we saw there was white smoke.
So, I stayed, hoping that the session would not begin, but
they began it all the same, and it was my turn to speak, as
the representative of the political block to which I belong,
about the referendum we had made concerning Las Malv-
inas² [the Falklands]. Before going to the bench, I said to
my advisors, "even though I will be talking, pass me a note
when you know the name of the new pope."

When I was actually talking about the Malvinas, I had
forgotten to turn off my cell phone, and I received several
calls from my husband, who knows that he should not call

² The Malvinas, called the "Falklands" by the British, are a group of islands
at the extreme south of the Atlantic Ocean located 290 miles to the east of
Argentina, claimed by Argentina as its territory but controlled by the United
Kingdom. The islands were the subject of an armed conflict that lasted from
April 2 to June 14, 1982. The British military victory caused the end of the
military dictatorship in Argentina. A few days after Pope Francis' election,
the inhabitants of the Malvinas held a referendum that reaffirmed their desire
to continue remaining part of the United Kingdom.

when I am in session. I turned off the phone, and I continued talking, and then I saw a text message from my daughter. In the Senate, they gave me a warning, and I told them: "Excuse me. I forgot to turn off my phone, but without a doubt by now the pope must have been named ... because if there is any person who is interested in knowing the name of the pope, that person is I."

While that was happening, someone said to me from behind: "Bergoglio"; I thought it was a joke, because we are an absolute minority, and there is not a whole lot of respect for what I think. I thought they wanted to make fun of me, but I asked, "Bergoglio?" and an advisor of mine came up to me with a tablet with the face of the cardinal. So, I said to the president: "Excuse me, I can't go on; I can't go on, I ask for a break." The majority leader yelled from his bench, "No! No!" But the president of the Senate told me, "Yes, it's okay Senator."

Suddenly, all the images of what we have been through hit me, because Cardinal Bergoglio was archbishop of the city of Buenos Aires. I tell you, I knew him when I was a senator; I have had three or four interviews with him, but the relationship deepened through the Parliamentarians and Governors for Life and Family. He participated in that congress, and he approached the [pro-life] Argentinean legislators to greet us, to encourage us to keep working, to have courage. And then the issue of same-sex marriage came up, which the Chamber of Deputies tried to pass quickly; and when it reached the National Senate, I was president of the commission.

So, with a few senators, we started to consider how we could make them listen to the Argentinean people, because this issue goes very much against the fundamental principles of our origins, of our values, of our roots, of our national identity. We could not believe what was happening to us.

As president of the commission, I raised the possibility of going out into the country. That had never happened in the National Senate, and so that is how it was that we went out to tour the Republic of Argentina. We started to listen to everyone; we went out to listen to families, to different sectors, even including those that were defending homosexual "marriage". We were very supported everywhere we went in this process, not only by Cardinal Bergoglio, but by the all the bishops of the Republic of Argentina.

*How do you remember Cardinal Bergoglio in this process?*

Cardinal Bergoglio was always a person who had a lot of courage and a lot of bravery to stand up before the powerful and say what he thought: Cardinal Bergoglio was the voice of those who did not have a voice. Especially in Buenos Aires, which was the place with the highest concentration of power, economic concentration, political concentration ... like we say, "God is everywhere, but his office is in Buenos Aires."

At this time, the president was Cristina Fernández, and her husband, the late ex-president Néstor Kirchner, was the national deputy. The future pope, in a *Te Deum* [Mass],[3] put forth two very strong theories about poverty and service. The presidential couple took it as a personal insult and decided never again to go to the *Te Deum*, and they began to travel to other dioceses in the Republic of Argentina in order not to have to face Cardinal Bergoglio.

On the issue of same-sex marriage, the Kirchners had pointed to Bergoglio as the enemy, because he understandably presented what the Church teaches in that respect. There

[3] The majority of Latin American countries have a *Te Deum* (we praise you) Mass on their national independence days, a celebration that usually takes place in the Catholic cathedral of the capital city.

was even a public rally in front of the Congress the afternoon before the approval of the law. That day, the cardinal sent a letter to the president of the Council for the Laity of the Archdiocese of Buenos Aires. The letter was read with his permission, and so the cardinal allowed his position to be publically known and encouraged the laity to continue working and fighting for our values.

The Kirchners said that the cardinal was coordinating the entire pro-family movement throughout Argentina. The cardinal also sent a letter to the Discalced Carmelites of Buenos Aires. I am not sure why, but the text started to circulate on the social networks: it contained not only a harsh criticism of the human catastrophe that the legalization of homosexual "marriage" would imply, but also asked that they pray for the illumination of the senators. On July 14, at ten in the morning, the debate began, which was very intense, and, without any break, it ended on July 15, when we lost the vote.

When we sat down to start the debate, we had had an advantage of nine votes, and in the end, we lost by three. So, you can tell how terrible that was. The ex-President Kirchner, as [honorary] national deputy, never went to the chamber. He went only twice: when he was sworn in as deputy . . . and when he voted in favor of same-sex "marriage".

*What was said about Cardinal Bergoglio in middle of the debate?*

I remember that a senator from the majority party interrupted the session to make a very harsh criticism of Cardinal Bergoglio and spoke about the letter he had sent to the Carmelites in Buenos Aires, in which the cardinal said, literally, "It is not a simple political fight; but rather an attempt to destroy the plan of God. It is not about a mere legislative project—that is only the instrument—but, rather, it is a 'move' by the father of lies, who intends to confuse and trick the children of God."

The letter said, in addition: "To the senators: cry out to the Lord for his Spirit to be sent to the senators who must vote. That they not be moved by error or by changing situations but, rather, according to what natural law and the law of God show us. This battle is not ours but God's. That they may assist, defend, and accompany us in God's will." [4] The senator from the majority who read this letter was [Marcelo] Fuentes, who used very harsh epithets against Cardinal Bergoglio. It was a moment of great tension because the session had many grievances.

I was president of the commission and, as such, had the "no" voice against homosexual "marriage". We had managed to agree on a bill that was supported by those who voted against same-sex marriage and that received, in addition, support for a civil union bill that was signed by eight of the fifteen senators. That is why we looked for eighty percent commitment of the members of the commission. In this group, there were Kirchnerist senators, provincial parties, the Radical Civic Union, and Peronism Federal Senators, to which I belong. The idea was to recognize some rights that same-sex cohabitants were asking for, such as, for example, a modification of the health care law, that they be allowed to go to the therapy of their partners, or the right to receive pensions.

That night, while there was a big rally outside the Senate and another letter from the cardinal was read—the one directed to the laity—by the president of the Senate, violating all the rules of procedure of the Argentinean Constitution, I was notified, as president of the commission, that it had been decided

---

[4] This paragraph is from Cardinal Jorge Bergoglio's letter to the Carmelite community of the Archdiocese of Buenos Aires, dated June 22, 2010, and was read during Senator Negre's interview.

to cancel the bill that had the support of 80 percent of the Senate and that the next day they would allow only a yes or a no vote on homosexual "marriage". The tension that existed became even stronger. The majority leader told me that I was a fascist, that I wanted to discriminate against homosexual persons like Hitler had done to the Jews, that I only needed to put on the swastika band. The situation made me cry, because I had been especially respectful, I had been very careful with my words. In the heat of the moment, during the early hours of the morning, I had to respond to all of these issues. But I especially wanted to refer to all the terrible things that had been said about the cardinal, whom nobody had defended.

I can read what I said, noting what Senator [Fuentes] was going to explain: "The Catholic Church corresponds to the Magisterium of the Church; that means that the Magisterium has a document, and that document was issued by the Catholic Church in 2005. The document has as its title: 'Considerations regarding Proposals to Give Legal Recognition to Unions between Homosexual Persons'. This is the position of the Catholic Church. So what Cardinal Bergoglio did when he drew up that letter addressed to the Carmelites, who are cloistered nuns, was to give an opinion in conformity with the internal norms of the Catholic Church."

"We must know how to differentiate between things and defend the ministers of religion. Yesterday Cardinal Bergoglio sent a letter to that march of laymen addressed to Dr. Carbajal, their president. That is one letter, and the one he sent to the Carmelites is another." I wanted to be clear that neither Cardinal Bergoglio nor other very valiant Argentinean bishops were "intervening in politics", as the majority party criticized, but rather he was reminding everyone, those who proclaim to be Catholic, what the Church teaches and was asking that these Catholics act accordingly.

*Let us go to the moment when you were informed in the Senate that the new pope was Cardinal Bergoglio ...*

When they told me "Bergoglio", at first I could not believe it because, in the first place, he had already presented his resignation here in Buenos Aires because he was already seventy-five years old. Besides, nobody in the media had mentioned him.

When I heard his name, and it was confirmed, all of these images came to mind because after they voted in favor of homosexual "marriage", the majority party said: "We brought down Bergoglio." They had regarded the fight for this law as if it were between them and Bergoglio. That is what the majority leader said. That is why I am so excited. I felt like "it had been written straight with a crooked line." I said to the Lord, "How you have rewarded him!" ... because he suffered in his own body the Calvary of our Lord.

Cardinal Bergoglio was reproached, insulted, defiled ... the things I heard during that twenty-four-hour session about the cardinal were unbelievable, and suddenly the Lord put him in that place as the Successor of Peter on earth. That is why I believe and say that he is a living martyr and is a hero. I could not continue my speech about Las Malvinas. I asked a colleague of mine, a senator from my political group, to replace me, and I went to my office and cried tears of joy, and I gave thanks to God.

*What happened after the announcement that Bergoglio had been elected pope?*

At that moment, the entire majority party was frozen; they were very surprised, unhappily surprised. Nobody from that group got up, but there were some who did and are from the opposition. When I finished talking, and despite the prohibition against applauding, booing, or yelling inside of the chamber, there was a standing ovation when I ended and left. All the advisors and a group of senators from the opposition came and greeted me. There were several of us who cried and felt a true joy. Now there is undoubtedly a change in the government party, the president that afternoon gave a very cold speech; she congratulated him very coldly. But it can be seen that later she reconsidered, and I have hope that she will have a more sincere attitude.

He also was very humble and gave proof of what he says: "Forgive and forget; carry the weight of the homeland on your shoulders; power is service." Everything he had told us in the family and in the documents he wrote, he gave witness to with the president [Cristina Fernández de Kirchner] because he asked her for fourteen audiences, and she never received him. Nevertheless, when she asked him for an audience, it was given, and she was received, for lunch together, for two hours—without press, without protocol, and without grudges.

I have a great hope that this wall will be able to fall between them and that it will be understood that the Catholic Church is really not against them. It is not the cardinal [Bergoglio] but rather the Church that has a mission to fulfill and has an obligation to illuminate the laity with the truth of her doctrine in order to be able to act, just as we have the obligation to vote in conformity with the Magisterium of the Church ... that is what I hope.

The president has now spoken of the "neighbor", a word she had never used before. I trust that this is going to pacify our spirits, since we are living in very harsh times of insecurity and political tension: with everyone against everyone, the poor against the poor, brothers against brothers ... and with this shocking news, we received something like balm for the soul.

The Argentineans and the political leaders, whoever they may be, will have to understand that now there is another figure to consider, because those of us who are practicing Catholics always follow the pope. Now, all Argentineans follow him, even though they do not share everything he says. He will never remain silent. He is always going to have a word, and he is going to guide us along the way.

The government has practically persecuted the Catholic Church, but now there is a great change, and I have great hope that this change will also be a change for us. I hope that all of this will cause us to reflect, to look beyond to the other person, to come out of our seclusion toward the periphery, as the Holy Father says, and learn to live more austerely and more modestly, thinking of those around me, and not so luxuriously. That is why I paid attention to the pope, and I did not travel to the inauguration of his pontificate, despite being named to his delegation. The money, as he asked, was donated to a project for the poor.

# Luisa Rosell

(professor of the Universidad del Salvador and friend of Pope Francis)

*How did you meet Pope Francis?*

I met him when our Pope Francis was the then-Father Jorge Mario Bergoglio, because the Universidad del Salvador was founded by the Jesuit Fathers, especially by two very praiseworthy priests, Father Ismael Quiles and Father Ernesto Dann Obregón. Father Bergoglio was then very young; he was close to Father Quiles. He visited him in his office at the Colegio del Salvador, which was the headquarters of the university, in the early days, and they had a very close relationship. Father Bergoglio was later elected provincial of the Society, he was precisely the one to whom the Father General of the Society, Pedro Arrupe, wrote a letter—we all later knew that—in which it states that he wanted to separate the Society of Jesus from the administration and supervision of the Universidad del Salvador. The reasons expressed in the letter for this decision had to do with the need for more pastoral works, among others. This occurred in 1974 and 1975. So, from that time on, those of us who formed part of the Universidad del Salvador were in direct and constant contact with Father Bergoglio. Members of the Society visited all the academic departments and informed us about how there was going to be a process that was called "decoupling". The university continued its close relationship with the Society, with the principles of the Society of

Jesus and with a vice-president of formation who was a Jesuit, Father Víctor Marangoni, until his death. During that period and as time passed, it was very common for Father Bergoglio to be at the board meetings and involved in the acts of the university.

In 1980, the first woman became president of a university in Argentina, Dr. María Mercedes Terrén, who is still living, although she is very elderly. Father Bergoglio did a great job there, in the sense of giving continuity and order.

It is striking that Father Bergoglio's words were always meaningful, drawing a line, indicating a concern, I would say a pastoral one, in all of his letters, and he did so in speaking to us academics. Also, many times he would direct his words to the entire university community.

*When the pope was appointed bishop, did he remain close to the university?*

We should remember that after the then archbishop of Buenos Aires, Archbishop Antonio Quarracino, promoted him, he was named auxiliary bishop, in charge of the Flores zone. And there again—and this I remember well, very vividly—he was speaking one day in the assembly hall in the Educational Science Department of the Universidad del Salvador. We were all there in a meeting, and he mentioned to us what he was doing, what his first days were like as a bishop, and he told us that he had received a very great and very beautiful house for being bishop. He had walked through it and found it full items like blankets and non-perishable food. So, what did he do? He went through the region where he was bishop, especially in Bajo Flores, where he knew the people, because that had been his childhood neighborhood. He saw the needs of the people, and he himself went back to hand out the things he had in his house.

This way of acting that we now see is not only that of the pope at present; rather, that came from the very moment he entered the Society of Jesus, when he was ordained a priest. There are some very beautiful words, in one of the magazines from the university, that in a tribute to Father Quiles review the virtues of the Jesuits, and the word that appears constantly is love.

The subject of letting oneself be found by God is constant. Also constant, for many years now, is his conviction that this letting oneself be found by God must bring one to meet one's neighbor. That is why when he was the auxiliary bishop, he decided to create an organization, the Lapacho Foundation, a tribute to the Lapacho tree, which is a native Argentinean tree with very beautiful flowers. He put it under the responsibility of Mrs. Ana Beta, whose husband—Dr. Enrique Beta—was the financial vice president of the university [del Salvador] until he passed away.

Ana did a lot of direct work with the poor, because Bishop Bergoglio did not want the foundation to be frivolous meeting centers, where they got together to play cards. I think I can still hear him say, very forcefully, when fundraising events were proposed that included some frivolous things: "That is not going to be, and that will not be done!" He did not like dinner or lunches or expensive suits. He did not associate that attitude with a Catholic foundation but, rather, wanted the Christian character of *caritas*, of freely given love, actually to be lived.

*What was the work of the Lapacho Foundation like?*

A short time ago, I saw a recording of something that Bishop Bergoglio was saying with respect to foundations or NGOs. He took the example of an important figure from Argentinean comics whose name is Mafalda. Who is Mafalda?

Mafalda is an imaginary person by a famous Argentinean cartoonist, Quino. Mafalda, this imaginary girl, is tremendous, a bit wise, with some very peculiar little friends. For example, a little boy who wants to be a shopkeeper and wants to earn a lot of money, little Susana, who wants to get married ... all really tremendous. So, one day little Susana says to her little friends that she wants to be big and make a lot of money so she can give many dinners, dances, and elegant meetings because then, with the money she would get—I will use the same words as little Susana—she could buy spaghetti and polenta "because that was the garbage poor people ate." Bishop Bergoglio did not want any Catholic to have a mind-set like that.[1] The Lapacho Foundation had a lot of very interesting cultural activity. I remember, for example, something that was routinely done but that had a very interesting characteristic. On Saturdays, they showed operas on giant screens in the assembly hall at the Universidad del Salvador. We paid our trifle, we learned, we heard the great voices of the opera. And that was done with a dual purpose: to educate and to raise money for the relief work.

*What were the encounters like with Pope Bergoglio?*

Following the death of Father Ismael Quiles in 1973, every July fourth the then-Bishop Bergoglio presided over the memorial Mass. There were two aspects to it: the Eucharist itself with a homily in which he used the same direct language he uses today and in which Father Quiles was remembered with affection. Sometimes he was very severe when he knew that something was not right in the university. He

---

[1] In the book *On Heaven and Earth*, a dialogue with Rabbi Abraham Skorka, Cardinal Bergoglio explicitly mentions the character of little Susana from the comic strip *Mafalda* as an example of how Catholic charity cannot be.

would say it with the same clarity we know today. He was kind of like a great watchtower, a guardian of the correct direction for the university. Later, what was interesting was the second part. After these Masses, we got together in the dean's office, back then that was Dr. Terrén, dean of the Education and Social Communications Department—I was the director of the College of Oriental Studies—and Bishop Bergoglio participated in a conversation that was only that, conversation. There was nothing else: no food, no drink, despite the fact that we Argentineans are inclined to drink or eat something when we talk. Nothing. It was truly a meeting to pay tribute to Quiles and with the presence of the already by that time Bishop Bergoglio. The conversations were wide-ranging, free, serious, but always austere.

Mingling there—and this is also very like him—were highly intellectual people from the most important families of the Republic of Argentina, who had greatly loved Father Quiles, and ambassadors were also present, among others. There were also very humble people who loved and had loved Father Quiles very much. Among these people, there was one person—I am sure Pope Francis remembers him very well— whose name was José, a very humble man, a laborer, who had a very large family. I knew José very well, and his wife, Isabel, who is still alive; they were service personnel from the university. Isabel always went to Father Quiles' Mass, with her husband, immaculate. They were both very humble.

Father Bergoglio is shorter than José, who was very tall. The pope would take his shoulder and introduce him to one after another, saying, "my friend José." Everyone, of course, greeted José fondly. But if there was a self-seeking careerist who wanted to take advantage of the opportunity to speak with Bishop Bergoglio and discuss some topic, it would be a complete failure. Everyone would see that. And there were often times when we had the opportunity to converse about some topic that was more social than religious, because this was the social part of the meeting. I continued calling him Father even though he was already bishop ... and it embarrassed me. I would say to him, "Hello, Father." I would say it without wanting to, because I was embarrassed, but he always laughed really hard at my absent-mindedness.

I also remember an employee of the university who had many children and whose husband died in a car accident. Bishop Bergoglio took care of getting her a job that would allow her to be with her children and take charge of them; he did it anonymously. We know because Mrs. Nora was a member of the university community, and she mentioned it. But we did not know this because Bishop Bergoglio had said, "I am doing this!"

*What was your relationship like with Bergoglio when he was then archbishop?*

He supported me a lot in the direction of the College of Oriental Studies, a task that was not easy. It is a complex job. The last time I saw him was for Dr. Beta's wake. As archbishop he had heard his confession and celebrated the funeral Mass. He stopped at the exit of the church and greeted everyone; like always, very simply. I approached him, greeted him, and thanked him for the Mass, and we spoke for about five minutes; he was always concerned for me, for the life of the university. After that, I only saw him in the assembly hall.

*What characteristic trait would you highlight about Pope Francis?*

The pope always had this constant concern for the other person. I believe that his life is inspired by the idea of *caritas*, by love. That is fundamental. In the academic life, for example, he encouraged great freedom. We never had blinders on, we were never closed, and there were no taboos. It was always clear that what was wrong, was wrong, but I mean the alleged social or fashionable taboos. I would also stress his austere and ascetic spiritual life. Faith and action are united, prayer and action. And later, straightforward language. When he told us what was wrong, he spelled it out, and in a very distinctive way that, I would say, sometimes included irony, with humor. He was very funny without being offensive and very quick mentally. That is what we see now, this colloquial language, as in the past. One time he used the word *trucho*, which in Argentinean slang means false. One day when the word was not yet very well known, he used it with complete simplicity, without doubts and without hesitation, and proceeded with a speech of a very high intellectual level. The cultured people who were present were very disconcerted. He had said *trucho* in the middle of a highly intellectual discourse!

*What was the experience like of discovering that he had been elected pope?*

Well, I was watching television, and when Cardinal Tauran said in Latin, "Jorge Mario", I said, "It can't be." Because he was the only Jorge Mario who was in the conclave. So I jumped up, and I started to call people on the phone. Everyone was happy, and we said to ourselves, "Do you remember when he came ... ? Do you remember this, or that, or the other ... ?"

Those memories touched me, deeply ... they bring back a lot of emotion ... I think, particularly, that this is going to be a great pontificate because he is a man with enormous firmness and charity. I say, in the good sense of the word, that he is made of steel. No one is going to lead him, no one is going to pressure him. Thanks be to God, he has great insight and is going to continue doing the same as he has done and the same as he is doing.

Of course, he is showing a renewal in continuity. In the serious work of government, as much religious as State, I believe he is going to be extremely decisive. He is going to be a very memorable pope who will benefit the entire Church and all human beings. I think what Father Quiles used to say when he started to work, "we must know the other half of humanity", will vibrate in him. Let us not forget that Saint Francis Xavier, a Jesuit saint who evangelized the Orient, died pointing toward China. The dear Pope Francis is a Jesuit with this comprehensive vision, open to the universal.

# Miguel Woites

(eighty-seven years old, director of the Agencia Informativa Católica Argentina [AICA] for fifty-seven years; collaborator of Cardinal Bergoglio)

*What has AICA's relationship been like with the archbishops of Buenos Aires?*

AICA is a Catholic news agency created by the Argentinean episcopate in 1956. In 1955, the Argentinean Church went through a very difficult time, which was called the persecution. Priests and bishops were imprisoned, the best churches in the center of Buenos Aires were set on fire ... and the Church did not have any means by which to communicate with the people. The bishops, who at that time were twenty-four—today there are more than seventy—met in a place located in the interior, Santa Rosa, and decided to create an information agency.

They may not have known much about what they were doing, but they did it. They came to Buenos Aires and sought someone to put in charge. Father Canales, who had recently come out of the seminary and was later auxiliary bishop of Buenos Aires, called me, and that is how we started in 1956. That makes fifty-seven years already. My appointment was made by Cardinal Antonio Caggiano, who was president of the episcopate and archbishop of Bueno Aires. Cardinal Antonio Quarracino reaffirmed it; and the last one to go back and reaffirm it was Cardinal Bergoglio. So, they have always left me here in this place without my having asked and without my having done anything. Cardinal Bergoglio once commented to some bishops around there, "While Woites is at the head, I am at ease" ... and well, here I am.

*What was your relationship like with Cardinal Bergoglio when he became archbishop of Buenos Aires?*

I knew him from when he was the auxiliary bishop, and I went to him a lot because when Cardinal Quarracino became sick, he was like my advisor. When he was archbishop, I consulted him about whatever problem I had, whatever was a bit difficult or doubtful: I picked up the phone, or I walked across the Plaza de Mayo,[1] and I saw him, and he always supported me in this job. Sometimes, there were very difficult things, for example, with other bishops or whatever it was, these things that occur in the Church, and he always gave me advice. In that way, a friendship was born, because we did not speak only about professional work.

*You had already known him when he was auxiliary bishop?*

When he came as auxiliary bishop, I started to work with him little by little, slowly. I knew the other auxiliary bishop, Bishop Héctor Aguer, better; but I did not know him as well. With the passing of time, we became friends, because I consulted him a lot. Cardinal Quarracino himself, with whom I had been very good friends since we were young, always told me, "Ask Bergoglio. He is going to solve your problems whenever you have them." And that is how it

---

[1] The Plaza de Mayo is the location of the headquarters of the Argentinean government and the cathedral of Buenos Aires; it is a couple of blocks away from the AICA offices in the center of the city.

was. I always went to him, and when he was coadjutor archbishop, even more so. I can say that we were friends.

*Can you read that passage that refers to you from the letter that Cardinal Bergoglio addressed to you in 2009 on the occasion of the AICA's anniversary?*

Well, it is a bit embarrassing . . . it says, "It would be unfair not to say a word about a person who has worked, for so many years, with this enthusiasm for communications in the Church and who has done it with perseverance and the conviction of a true mission. However, what impresses me most about you is your life witness. It not only impresses me, but it is good for my soul."

Many times when I consulted him or when I went there personally, in addition to the times I consulted him about an issue, he would come to me, for example, with a passage from the Gospel or the Fathers of the Church or a spiritual letter, and we chatted about spirituality; sometimes for a long time.

He had a very intense spiritual life. Many times when I went to see him in his office, he was not there; he was walking the halls praying his rosary or was in the little chapel that is in the Curia, praying before the Blessed Sacrament. I saw him do that so many times. Almost no one speaks about his interior life, and that really edified me. He says that I edified him, well, it was something mutual.

*Was Bergoglio the person that the press has often described as being caught up in politics?*

Well, in the first place, he never intervened in politics, that is the truth. Journalists interpreted some of his remarks as allusions to politics, which is another thing. For example, the press always brings up that famous homily at the *Te Deum* before the presidential couple [The Kirchners], where he said, "Carry the weight of Argentina on your shoulders" ... but he was saying that to everyone, not only to the government. He spoke to everyone as the pastor he was; he did not make exceptions, nor were his thoughts on political things.

He was interested in the social situation of the poor, of the elderly, of children, that was his great concern, which at times journalists interpreted differently. Many times the press concentrated on subjects like Latin in the Mass or marriage for priests, things that, sometimes, were of secondary importance. When Pope Francis would say something, they were all immediately looking for some word by which to manipulate his declarations or to interpret as they pleased.

*The pope presided at the Mass for your golden wedding anniversary.*

When we celebrated our golden anniversary, I organized a Mass in my parish, which is the Basilica of the Sagrado Corazón, a very large church, and I invited some priest friends and some bishop friends. A bishop friend of mine, who is now deceased, was going to preside, a friend of the family, very close, a great priest, but as a matter of protocol I went and told Cardinal Bergoglio about the Mass.

I said him, "Look, this day we are going to have an anniversary Mass, and I have come to tell you that the nuncio is going to participate." After he had listened to me, with much humility, timidly, and even with a little fear, he said to me, "You do not want me to preside over it?" He almost asked me if he could please preside. "Why not!" And, well, he presided over it, and we celebrated with fifteen bishops and more than thirty priests. It was an event, something I did not deserve ... but that is how it was, and it started a kind of revolution in the neighborhood where I live. One bishop there even joked, saying that more bishops went to my anniversary Mass than to an episcopal ordination.

*Why did Pope Francis send you a personal letter recently?*

A short time ago I celebrated sixty years of marriage. Only the family went to the Mass we celebrated in the nunciature: father, mother, children, grandchildren, and great-grandchildren. There were fifty-four of us without a single person invited besides the family. The nuncio began by remembering that ten years earlier, Cardinal Bergoglio had presided over our golden anniversary Mass, but he could not come from Rome, so as nuncio and representative of the pope, he would preside over it.

He gave us the chapel inside the nunciature for the celebration. To my surprise, the nuncio had a personal letter for us from Pope Francis. It said:

Dear Don Miguel [he always said that to me, Don Miguel], I received your letter. Through these words I want to make my heart present at the Mass on the first of April. I will pray with you and with Lidia, giving thanks for these sixty very blessed years of your domestic Church, for your children, five children, twenty-seven grandchildren, and seven great-grandchildren, thanking you for your witness to the search for holiness that you have given me. Thank you for having loved and for continuing to love the Church and for expressing this love with an exemplary married life.

To you, to your wife, children, grandchildren, and great-grandchildren, I send my blessing on this very joyful day, and please, I ask you not to forget to pray and to pray for me.

May Jesus bless you and the Holy Mother care for you.

A very beautiful letter in which he insists, very strongly, that I am an example for him ... no, I do not think that would be the truth; I believe that speaks, rather, of his humility and his sensitivity.

*What do you believe is going to most attract attention about Pope Francis in the immediate future?*

First, his simplicity, which is already drawing attention, his detachment from luxury and comfort, and his very intense concern for the poor, for people who suffer. The selection of the name Francis confirms his concern for the poor, because it truly is a very profound feeling in him.

He does not say it to appear or look good with the poor. No. He just did it like that, and he went secretly to visit them, without boasting, without proclaiming it to the four winds. Now many things are being discovered, and many say, "Ah, yes, he came to visit my slum, he came here." He is another Francis, another Saint Francis. Lately, and from the altar, he has also repeated several times: "Go outside. Let us not stay in the Church, in the sacristy, go out!" He has a little word he always uses: "To the periphery". Now he also says it in the Holy See: "We have to go out toward the periphery because that is there where the people are who need our word, the people who need the message of the Gospel."

The periphery is periphery in every sense, not only in the physical, but also in the spiritual. That periphery of the people who are far from the Church, the periphery of the people who are socially considered least, that is also the periphery that can be right here in the center of Buenos Aires.

To the young people of Catholic Action, to youth in general, he would send them to the center, to the streets, to the neighborhoods, to the plazas, there, physically, to take action, to speak, as our Protestant friends sometimes do. I believe he is doing the same thing, but this time with the youth of the world. We have to "go out of the church and go out of the sacristy!"

# José María Poirier

(journalist and director of the Catholic magazine *Criterio* since 1996. He interviewed the then Archbishop Bergoglio several times)

*What do you know about the family of Pope Francis?*

He always remembers his family, and that is in the book *El Jesuita*, and more than once he commented about it. He remembered, above all, his grandparents, because being the oldest sibling, who stayed to take care of his mother, with the grandparents living close by, he—as a boy—many times was with his grandparents and always remembers his grandmother as the woman who taught him to pray, who brought him closer to the religious dimension.

He had a great appreciation for his father; I believe he considered him a figure who marked his family life. To help his family, he studied chemistry, not in the university, but on a technical level, as an occupational option, but he was always attracted to literature and philosophy.

One day he told that he had a short courtship, but afterward he made the decision to be a priest. But he always remained very close to his family. For example, the death of his brother hit him very hard. I remember that he mentioned it to me with great sorrow, because his brother died when he was already cardinal of Buenos Aires. He maintained a close relationship with his sisters, whom he always calls on the phone.

*Tell us how you met Cardinal Jorge Mario Bergoglio.*

The first time I had the pleasure of meeting and greeting him was when I was introduced by two bishops, one of whom has now passed away, Bishop Justo Laguna, and the other was Bishop Jorge Casaretto, who was bishop of San Isidro until a short time ago and is still very active in "Social Pastoral". It was the occasion of a meeting with the then President Raúl Alfonsín, and I was introduced to Jorge Bergoglio, who at that time was still the superior of the Jesuits in Argentina, a very discreet man, very quiet, very serious, who exchanged few words, in general, with those around him. I went back to deal with him when he was the auxiliary bishop of Buenos Aires. Later, he was coadjutor, and it was known that at the resignation or the death of Cardinal Quarracino, he was going to be his successor, which in fact happened in 1998. When he became archbishop of Buenos Aires, I proposed during the editorial meeting of *Criterio*, before the council, that we invite him to talk, since we were in his diocese.

Not everyone agreed, because the tradition at *Criterio* was to always maintain a distance in dealing with bishops and, above all, the bishop of this archdiocese, so as to preserve critical freedom. But finally the majority said that it would not displease us to have a meeting with him in order to know him better.

The editorial council meetings are traditionally on Tuesdays during the evening, at six o'clock sharp. I went to see him, to invite him; he accepted, and we set a date. It was during the winter, and that day the city appeared to be flooded. Nevertheless, showing his punctuality, Bergoglio arrived a 6 P.M. in this very office ... and almost no member of the editorial council had yet arrived because the entire world was in the middle of the storm. Bergoglio had come on foot from his house beside the cathedral. The two or three who had arrived apologized, saying that the others were about to arrive, and he said, "Yes, of course. Do not be nervous, we will wait for them and drink some maté." He always treats other people like family. Little by little, almost twenty people arrived, all drenched . . . and he was very friendly in the discussion that day in which we talked about a political editorial.

He refused to accept a place of honor; he remained where he was and asked that we allow him to share his opinion, "I know that I do not have the right to vote, because I am not part of the magazine, but I would be interested in debating the political issue", and he participated actively, saying what he agreed with and what he did not. He was very nice and was very thankful for that invitation and said that each person fulfills a role in the life of the Church and the life of her institutions.

*How did the relationship with him continue?*

Some incidents, very typical of the personality of Jorge Mario Bergoglio, followed, for example, when he called me at my house one Saturday afternoon. He introduced himself saying, "It's Bergoglio, and I want to speak to such and such a person." That surprised me. He was already cardinal then and wanted to comment on something in the magazine or exchange public opinions. They were very friendly conversations, and, afterward, one knew that it was common for him to call people at the most informal times to talk. It was also a form of strengthening relationships; Bergoglio was always a man with a low profile, but very decisive, who knew how to weave a myriad of relationships with all types of people in Buenos Aires, in the country, and in the last years on a Latin American level.

On one occasion after the conclave that elected Pope Benedict XVI, I had to travel to Bogotá [Colombia] for a CELAM [Latin American Episcopal Council] meeting to which journalists were invited from different Latin American countries, and I met an English journalist there who had traveled a lot through Latin America, and he asked me that night to write an article about Bergoglio now that he had supposedly received some votes in the conclave and nobody knew who he was.

That night I had to write an article, and I remember it occurred to me to start by saying, "What does Cardinal Bergoglio think? Nobody knows." I believe that was always the key to his great kindness, his being very gracious, but always keeping somewhat "secret" the complexity of his thought, above all on important issues.

That article was published, and not long after I found myself with Cardinal Bergoglio at the presentation of a book. When he greeted me, he said, "So no one knows what I think?" and he started laughing. I was also surprised. He was always an attentive reader of newspapers, magazines, and information in general.

One thing that caught my attention and is surprising is that he handles so much information and has such a prodigious memory. Francesca Ambrogetti, the co-author of the book *El Jesuita*, told me he gave her some information for an article, and she thanked him very much, saying to him that that day was her birthday. To her surprise, the next year Bergoglio called her on the phone to wish her a happy birthday again. That was a characteristic he always had: personal relationships, a great memory, and great confidence in his notebook.

Upon having submitted his resignation, he had already arranged to take a room in the residence for priests in the Flores neighborhood, which was his original neighborhood and which is a place with which he was much concerned, where there are elderly and sick priests. He went very diligently to visit them, and he had arranged to have a room there, like any other elderly priest, for whenever the pope accepted his resignation. Some say that he knew very clearly what he would do if he were elected pope, and I believe that is true, because I believe that Bergoglio is essentially a political man, in the classical sense of the word. Meaning, one has the impression that he has studied all the scenarios. Bergoglio knew what to do if he had to withdraw and retire; Bergoglio knew what to do if he had to continue as archbishop of Buenos Aires, and—why not?—he had also thought about what to do if they elected him pope.

*What can you say of the accusations about his supposed link with the dictatorship?*

Well, about that situation in particular, there is this rancor on the part of an important Argentinean journalist, Horacio Verbitsky, who manages information about the Church very well. He always considered himself an agnostic; he has devoted many years to the inner workings of Argentinean Church politics and has written several books with very good information but also with many hypotheses or many conclusions that he bases on words or silences.

Everyone knows he never got along well with Bergoglio. Why? Well, it would be complex to analyze, particularly because they have two very divergent visions of Peronist political phenomena. Horacio Verbitsky has a leftist perspective, from the Montoneros group, which was the extreme left of Peronism.[1] Bergoglio in his youth was sympathetic

---

[1] The Montoneros were a guerrilla group whose acts of terrorism triggered the 1976 military coup.

to "orthodox" Peronism, which had moved away from Marxism. So, the same political phenomena can be interpreted in very different ways even from a Peronist perspective. Moreover, his status as a Jesuit was always problematic for Verbitsky, who never understood and had suspicions about the nature of the Jesuits.

During the years of the military dictatorship, Bergoglio was a young provincial superior, and today there is testimony from many people, among them priests, who say, "he saved my life, he protected me, he drove me, he hid me, and he helped me leave the country." In the Verbitsky case, he is referring to two Jesuit priests, Orlando Yorio and Francisco Jalics.

They did not agree with the directive Bergoglio gave as provincial that they had to withdraw from the place where they were because he could not guarantee their safety in the face of the kidnappings during the military dictatorship. They, however, disagreed and preferred to disobey in order to continue their pastoral and political action where they were. A short time later they were kidnapped, imprisoned, and tortured by military forces.

Bergoglio was one of the most active in trying to get them out and even had meetings with some military commanders asking for those two priests, who finally, after some months, reappeared and were accompanied by Bergoglio and by Bishop Jorge Novak, then bishop of Quilmes, to the airport, in order to travel to Europe and save their lives.

I had the opportunity, some years ago, to write a book about Bishop Novak, who was a strict defender of human rights, even confronting a large part of the Argentinean episcopate, whom he accused of having opted for silence or for private dealings, when he maintained that the denunciations ought to be public and should confront the military dictatorship's government.

Accusations of this type and on other subjects also have their origin in the fact that Néstor and Cristina Kirchner[2] always saw Bergoglio as a public enemy. I believe that the president [Cristina Fernández de Kirchner] realized later that she had the wrong enemy, because when it was announced that Bergoglio was the new Pope Francis, the response was very difficult for the government.

The government had bet on any other candidate, but not on this one, whom they had regarded as already defeated. The first reaction of the government was very uncomfortable, very cold, without managing to come up with anything to say, and only a day and a half later, the president made a political U-turn and showed some support for this Argentinean pope. Of course, the new pope rose to the occasion with his response, because he immediately invited her and had this meeting where he demonstrated his great kindness.

What did they talk about during those two hours? We are not going to know, but certainly it was a meeting between two people with great political acumen, even though far apart in their vision of how things in this country ought to be addressed.

Some intellectuals very close to the government remained very disoriented, very lost, but well, those are the costs that must be paid for political militancy. The government has already decided to change its strategy and capitalize on an Argentinean pope instead of struggling with him.

---

[2] Néstor Carlos Kirchner (1950–2010) was an Argentinean politician, lawyer, and businessman who was elected president of Argentina in 2003 and governed the country until 2007. His wife, Cristina, succeeded him as President of Argentina.

*What do you believe are the most salient qualities of Pope Francis?*

I think he has kept great personal consistency and at the same time kept a low profile. I believe that was a conscious choice. He knew that he was uncomfortable politically with the government, that he was not entirely comfortable with some ultraconservative sectors of the Church and even some bishops.

He is a man who is orthodox in doctrine and very moderate; he is a man of great social sensitivity and deeply pastoral.

Bergoglio is a priest who, in confronting a problem, sees the person and develops the pastoral ministry on the basis of the person, of the situation, and that has given him great flexibility, and that is why he is so loved by his priests and by many people, especially the humble, who, always found him a pastor who was close to them.

We have all seen him on the streets of Buenos Aires. I have seen him in the subway, in the metro, more than once we exchanged some remarks. He was a man who never had a car when he was archbishop and would never agree to take a taxi or be driven anywhere because he would say, "Public transportation allows me to meet people and understand what they are living."

Furthermore, he was, he is, an absolutely austere man. He lived very frugally in the Curia, and on weekends when he was alone, he cooked for himself; he organized his life, and every weekend he went to visit outlying parishes. Fundamentally, parishes in humble, working-class neighborhoods, and in slums, which were his priority.

The priests who worked and lived in the slums were always the priority of Bergoglio. Bergoglio had a phrase that he used more than once, "The Church has to go out to the frontiers", and that is why he would say to the priests, "You do not have to call people to the church; rather, you must go out to where the people are."

When the magazine *Criterio* marked eighty years, he wanted to celebrate a Mass, and he told us, "If I can give you some advice: be on the cultural frontiers, do not expect the intellectuals to come to you; you be the ones go out to meet the non-religious intellectuals, the non-Catholics and non-Christians."

That was very much in evidence, for example, in his productive ecumenical and interreligious dealings, his friendship with rabbis, with pastors, with members of the Islamic community. The paradox is that, despite this great activity, having opted for such a low profile, he was almost invisible in the eyes of the city.

*What was the archbishop like in relation to the most needy?*

Bergoglio always said that the poor and the people in the street, those who—according to him—are "on the side of the road" become invisible. That pained Bergoglio, and he pointed out that "we end up not seeing them; they form part of a faceless message." He worried because he wanted us to open our eyes to take them into account in every circumstance.

We were surprised that he was made pope and that a vast number of testimonies of friendship appeared, from the street sweeper who knew him, from the paperboy whom he phoned to tell him to stop the delivery of his newspaper, "because I have to stay in Rome", or from the many other humble people who had had constant dealings with him.

One of those people said that he was very far removed from the life of the Church; he found himself in a very difficult situation, and he with his communist wife had camped out in the Plaza de Mayo[3] with one of his children to protest. One day Bergoglio passed by and greeted them. Bergoglio always dressed as a simple clergyman, and I do not know if people recognized that he was a cardinal, but at least they knew he was a priest who passed by. The man greeted him, introduced himself, and said to him, "Look, I wanted to speak with you as bishop to tell you many things that are concerning us", and he said, "Why do you not come and visit me the day after tomorrow?" The man responded, "I do not want another person to see me, I want to speak with you." This man says that in fact the cardinal came down to receive him, and they spoke. He told him about his economic difficulties and that he was not able to pay rent on the home where he was living.

Bergoglio took an interest in the case and told him, "I can help you, I can pay your rent; I am going to get a house, and I am going to pay the rent for three years, but during those three years you have to promise that you will finish high school, get a job, and send your children to school, that is the deal." Apparently every weekend he phoned him to see how his children were doing in school, how he was doing, and if he was in fact fulfilling his promise. He graduated, got a job, and was able to pay the rent.

That is Bergoglio's idea of social promotion. He is very attentive to the dignity of the person and felt that many of the social plans put forth by governments did not take this into account. They are aid programs in return for political votes and keep the poor submerged in their inability to act as worthy people, as citizens. That is the great difference. Many of us wonder how he is going to be able to be with people as the bishop of Rome, it will be a great security

[3] The main square of the city of Buenos Aires, the site of the presidential headquarters, the Casa Rosada.

problem, for the entire system ... but he is not going to waver in his constant need for direct contact with people.

*What can you tell us about his capacity to make decisions?*

I am convinced and I believe that he is a man of authority who understands very clearly some of the very great difficulties of the Church. In the first place, for example, he always agreed with applying Benedict XVI's line of zero tolerance with regard to sexual abuse of minors by the clergy and the involvement of the legal system in the different countries, because this is a crime. Bergoglio always distinguished very well between weakness, sin, and crime. He explained that if a priest is celibate and has promised to remain that way, living in a relationship with a woman—of legal age—is a weakness, and for a priest that is a sin, but it is not a crime. It is a crime to steal, to abuse minors, to commit illicit acts, and on that he has always been very, very clear. That has made it possible for him to help many people. He was tough on crime, but was very sympathetic with weakness and sin. He is a great confessor; he is a man who is very used to that.

The second important theme for him, in terms of government, is the search for financial transparency in the Church. He was bothered enormously by the mistakes in the management of the Vatican bank. That lack of transparency is something he does not support because he was a very attentive administrator at the Archdiocese of Buenos Aires; he wanted a lot of austerity and transparency in the accounts.

The third theme, I believe, is the thorough reform of the Roman Curia, of which he knows many things and with which he has had many clashes. I mean, he did not agree with a Curia that became, during the last long years of John Paul II's illness, an autonomous and parallel government, of which he certainly did not approve. That Curia, in reality, instead of serving as a link between the bishops and the pope, became an impediment to that relationship. So, I believe Bergoglio is going to work on these three points and is going to demonstrate that he is a Jesuit who is in control, who has authority, and who wants that authority to be respected.

He is adamant on this point. Afterward, there are the *ad extra* issues, and Bergoglio is aware that the Church has lost a lot of time and a lot of presence and that the rehabilitation of the Church in society depends on her consistency in the virtues. He wants a holy Church, or at least one with a great striving for virtue, and that virtue has to be demonstrated particularly in poverty, which is why he chose the name Francis. He is a man with great ecological sensitivity; he believes that this respect, this care that we owe as people, must also be manifested in creation, in nature. On the other hand, I do not think that Bergoglio wants to make many trips; I believe that difficulties of his age and health make travel unappealing. He also thinks he can accomplish something through the media, as he has shown during these first weeks. I believe he wants to establish a presence so that he can be with people where they are, in concrete situations.

*You presented the book* On Heaven and Earth;[4] *what do you believe its impact has been?*

Pope Francis, I believe, has very clear ideas about the relationship between Christianity and Judaism, which is a preferential relationship because, using an expression from John

---

[4] *On Heaven and Earth* is a book of conversations between the then archbishop of Buenos Aires, Cardinal Jorge Mario Bergoglio, and the president of the Rabbinic School of Latin America, Rabbi Abraham Skorka.

Paul II, the Jews are our older brothers in the faith. Bergoglio very clearly felt this and was able to establish a great friendship with many rabbis and Jewish leaders, religious and non-religious, and that was very curious. The only time he suggested a name for me to contact for an article, I thought he was going to say either some priest or some Catholic intellectual, but he gave me the name of a Jewish agnostic intellectual. He told me, "Excellent person, ask him for an article if you can."

Last night in the synagogue on Libertad Street, the rabbi spoke and Representative Sergio Bergman, who went to greet the pope in Rome. He related that Bergoglio told him, "How did you manage to get inside here?" And he laughed.

Bergman gave a very powerful testimony, because he said, "I have to speak only in Christian terms this night because my political and spiritual reference has always been the great Rabbi Bergoglio." People were very surprised at what they heard, and later he said, "because you must read the bishops' documents more closely, know the history of the Church and especially that of the Society of Jesus." He gave a master class on the history of the Church, explaining that if that is important for a Jew, how much more so it must be for a Catholic. That was always a very original ability of Bergoglio, to establish ties with Rabbi Abraham Skorka, who is a very important rabbi for the Jewish world and for interreligious dialogue in Argentina.

The two established a relationship marked by so much affection and confidence that they have had many programs where they gave spirituality classes on television, and finally they wrote this book [*On Heaven and Earth*], but the curious thing is that they agreed that Bergoglio would choose who from the Jewish world was going to present the book, and the rabbi agreed to choose who from the Catholic world would present it. It was Skorka who asked me to present the book. The presentation was very nice; Bergoglio came up to me and said to me, "I am giving you work, and I apologize." And I said to him, "It was a pleasure for me to come." He always played with those very nice expressions.

Here, he always spoke a very *porteño* Spanish, very much from Buenos Aires, a little old-fashioned, with expressions from lyrics taken from tangos, from writers of past decades, which allowed him to be friendly without falling into the ambiguity of a very common language. He had a very curious thing in his way of speaking, it was as if he were searching for words that sounded familiar but were also old in order to protect himself. In this sense, he was very charming, and he gave me complete freedom to review the book, which is a great testimony of the brotherhood between the two of them. I know the two accepted advice from each other; the book was presented that time in the Latin American Rabbinic Seminary. So, there was a large Jewish community and a large Christian community present. Bergoglio said a few things, the rabbi was much more expressive. Bergoglio, it is very curious, in Buenos Aires, always spoke with a low voice; today we suspect that he did it to force us to be attentive, because as soon as he was named pope, he spoke with a strong voice.

We had always seen him very serious, as if he were very worried; he appeared on the balcony in front of St. Peter's square smiling, and he kept smiling. This means there has been a curious change, at least in his way of presenting himself.

Bergoglio always conveys the confidence of someone who knows where he stands, knows what he wants to do, where he is headed, even though he will not tell you explicitly. He left a great many memories of himself here with the Jewish community and a certain nostalgia in his absence.

Today I read a letter he sent yesterday to the mayor of Buenos Aires, to the head of the city government, and among other things he said to him that now when he remembers his work in Buenos Aires, the first thing that comes to mind are the endless faces, the faces of many children, of the elderly, of young people with dreams, of marriages with difficulties, and of the poor. With that letter, he also spoke indirectly to the national political power, asking that they respect the dignity of all people.

That has always distinguished Bergoglio, a great Jesuit, a man of excellent formation. He is a man of action, of leadership, and of exceptional political tact. I do not think he is an intellectual, because, while he had a very good education, he is not a man really immersed in academia—work that he respects very much—because that was not his priority. His priority was pastoral action.

*Do you have some memory that has marked your relationship with Pope Francis?*

In one of the first meetings he had with me, his office was excessively modest, because it was uncomfortable. I mean you had to open the door, move a chair in order to close it, and then move the chair back to its place. It was like a lesson in austerity that he was constantly giving. Moreover, he had very few books, very few papers, did not use the computer; he liked soccer a lot, but he sometimes listened to the games on the radio, and that is a rather outdated thing to do.

When he said goodbye to me that time, he said to me, "I will go with you to the exit", and I said to him, "Do not bother", and he responded, "It is no bother, I like doing it." He asked me if he could do something more for me, and I could not think of anything, so I asked him for a blessing for myself, for the activities of the magazine, and for the culture. "That is a good request", he told me; so as a good Jesuit he gave me a blessing that also expressed an intense spirituality.

I also remember that when a great French Jesuit died in Paris, Jean-Yves Calvez, who came every year to Buenos Aires, Bergoglio phoned me and said me, "I know you regarded him highly, and, though I did not agree with many of Calvez's ideas, I always admired his depth and his goodness; he was a holy man."

Rabbi Skorka always remembers Bergoglio's closeness when he lost a very dear relative. In other words, the kind gestures of Bergoglio were always very evident. On another occasion, leaving late from a meeting with Cardinal Bergoglio, he proposed they return to the center by taxi, but he told him, no, and on that subject he did not waver. It was a principle of his not to let anyone pick him up because it seemed to him to set him apart, and, moreover, he needed the daily and constant contact with people.

We went back in the subway, and at that time of night there were young people listening to their music or tired people, and he would gaze at them, as if praying for them, because he looked at them deeply, in silence. What is life like for a young person with abilities but no work prospects, no way of getting ahead or hope?

He has always been and will always be an exceptional pastor.